Chain of Tears

Chain of Tears
Selling Our Daughters

KRISTINE OHKUBO

Copyright © 2023 by Kristine Ohkubo.

All rights reserved. No part of this publication may be reproduced, distributed, or transmitted in any form or by any means, including photocopying, recording, or other electronic or mechanical methods, without the prior written permission of the author, except in the case of brief quotations embodied in critical reviews and certain other noncommercial uses permitted by copyright law. For permission requests, contact the author using the website address provided below.

https://kristineohkubo.wixsite.com/nonfiction-author

Chain of Tears: *Selling Our Daughters* /Kristine Ohkubo. —1st ed.

ISBN 979-8-8692-1947-3

Table of Contents

Introduction 1
Sex and Marriage in Premodern Japan 7
Aruki Miko 13
Izumo no Okuni 17
The Asobi 23
The Shirabyoshi 31
Prostitution During the Edo Period 37
Yoshiwara: Tokyo's Red-Light District 45
The Yoshiwara Arson Incident 54
The Yoshiwara Killing Spree 60
Jokan-ji: The Throwaway Temple 62
Shimabara: Kyoto's Red-Light District 66
Shinmachi: Osaka's Red-Light District 70
Furuichi: Ise's Red-Light District 73
The Abura-ya Riot 78
Dairin-ji Temple 81
Maruyama: Nagasaki's Red-Light District 84
Life of a Courtesan 98
The Kamuro 106
The Oiran 112
Takao Dayu II 120
Usugumo Dayu 125
Yoshino Dayu II 128
Katsuyama Dayu 130
Komurasaki Dayu 132
Ohashi Dayu 133
Sakuragi Dayu 134

Yugiri Dayu I 136

Yachiyo Dayu 137

Karayuki 141

Yamada Waka 146

Orandayuki 149

Kusumoto Taki 154

Jigoku Dayu: Hell Courtesan 157

Kagema: The Male Sex Workers 163

Prostitution During the Meiji Period and Beyond 169

The Comfort Women 180

Prostitution Prevention Law 189

Glossary 193

List of Illustrations 200

Works Cited 203

About the Author 212

"The women in the village told them, 'If you go to Yoshiwara, you'll be able to eat white rice every day and wear beautiful kimonos,' and their parents told them, 'Think of this as filial piety and endure it.' While being told many things, the young girls were sold to Yoshiwara with tears in their eyes."[1]

---

[1] "梅毒に感染も。江戸時代における遊女の一生が過酷すぎる【写真あり】| 江戸ガイド ("Also Infected with Syphilis. The Life of a Prostitute in the Edo Period Was Extremely Harsh [with Photos]." | Edo Guide)." 江戸ガイド, 江戸ガイド, 9 Apr. 2022, edo-g.com/blog/2016/02/yujo.html.

i. A kamuro having makeup applied,. Photo by Yoshiro Miyazaki. Public domain.

Introduction

Prostitution is widely recognized as one of the oldest professions in human history, going back to the 24th century BCE. During that period, the ancient Near East was home to numerous *houses of heaven* [2] where *sacred prostitution* [3] was practiced. Over the course of history, the practice of sacred prostitution gradually spread to other parts of the world, including Greece, Italy, India, China, and Japan.[4]

In Japan, numerous shrines and temples that employed *miko* (shrine maidens) fell on hard times during the Kamakura period (1185–1333) —a time of significant conflict and the rise of feudalism in the country. Some of the miko who were compelled to live as vagrants turned to prostitution as means of survival.[5]

Prostitution as a profession has endured throughout the course of Japan's history. Liberal interpretations, loose enforcement, and loopholes in the *Prostitution Prevention Law of 1956*, which prohibits both involvement in prostitution and patronage thereof,[6] have enabled the Japanese sex

---

[2] "History of Prostitution." Wikipedia, Wikimedia Foundation, 15 Mar. 2023, https://en.wikipedia.org/wiki/History_of_prostitution#:~:text=Ancient%20Near%20East,-See%20also%3A%20Sacred&text=2400%20BCE%20are%20the%20earliest,in%20the%20city%20of%20Uruk..
[3] Paid intercourse performed in the context of religious worship. "Sacred Prostitution." Wikipedia, Wikimedia Foundation, 15 Feb. 2023, https://en.wikipedia.org/wiki/Sacred_prostitution.
[4] "History of Prostitution." Wikipedia, Wikimedia Foundation. https://en.wikipedia.org/wiki/History_of_prostitution
[5] Writers, YABAI. "Miko: The Shrine Maidens of Japan-" YABAI, 27 June 2017, http://yabai.com/p/2317.
[6] "Prostitution in Japan." Wikipedia, Wikimedia Foundation, 28 Dec. 2022, https://en.wikipedia.org/wiki/Prostitution_in_Japan.

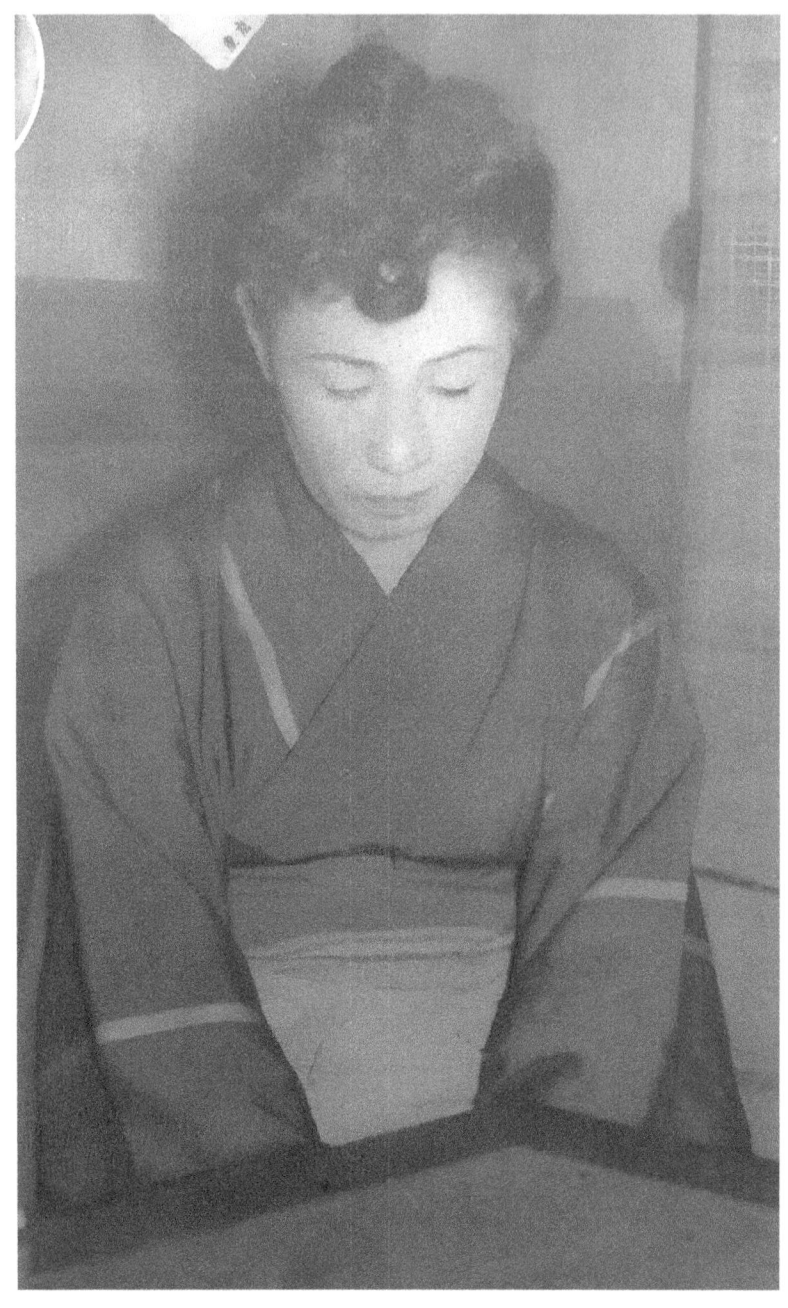

ii. Abe Sada, circa 1947. Public domain

industry to flourish and generate an estimated 2.3 trillion yen ($24 billion) annually in revenue. This places the sex industry in Japan as the third largest globally, following China ($73 billion) and Spain ($26.5 billion).[7]

While doing research for my third book, *Nickname Flower of Evil (呼び名は悪の花): The Abe Sada Story (2019)*, I was shocked to discover that Sada and her older sister were sold to brothel owners by their father as a form of punishment. During the Edo period (1603-1868), prostitution in Japan was licensed and subsequently legalized. It was not uncommon for destitute families to sell their daughters into indentured servitude within the sex industry to obtain the cash advances that were essential for the family's survival. Samurai families also engaged in the practice of selling their wayward daughters as a means of punishment.

Girls were usually procured from fishing villages, impoverished rural provinces, and the residences of low-ranking samurai families. Occasionally, merchant families in financial trouble sold their daughters in order to repay their debts. Every now and then, a young girl was duped by an unscrupulous man and sold to a *zegen* (someone who makes their living selling women into prostitution).

Parents were provided with a lump sum of cash in consideration of their daughters' future earning potential. The sum of money given to the parents differed in accordance with the girl's lineage. Typically, three to five ryo (equivalent to 300,000 to 500,000 yen today or $2,400 to $3,400) were paid for a girl from a rural family. If the girl came from a low-

---

[7] Keohan, Matt. "These Are the Top 10 Countries That Spend the Most on Prostitutes." BroBible, 13 Oct. 2022, brobible.com/life/article/top-10-countries-spend-most-prostitutes/.

ranking samurai family, she would usually command eighteen ryo (equivalent to 1.8 million yen or $12,000).[8]

Following the legalization of prostitution by the *shogunate* (the military government of Japan during the Edo period), designated red-light districts were established near major cities such as Edo (present-day Tokyo), Kyoto, Osaka, and Nagasaki. In time, the government sanctioned illicit brothels, arresting the women employed there and selling them at auctions to brothels operating within the authorized pleasure quarters. Due to the prohibition of human trafficking by the shogunate, the women involved in prostitution within the approved quarters were commonly referred to as "servants" rather than prostitutes.

Despite the negative societal perception of prostitutes, the practice of selling daughters was not condemned in Japanese society on the grounds that the girls were merely performing their filial obligation.

A significant number of female workers in the sex industry were indentured to brothels when they were young, typically between seven and nine years old. Brothel purveyors would commonly crisscross impoverished rural communities and fishing villages during the spring, when food rations were scarce, and the summer, when taxes were due. While the girls were generally enslaved for a duration of ten years, the indebtedness they incurred as prostitutes relegated them to that lifestyle indefinitely.[9]

---

[8] "梅毒に感染も。江戸時代における遊女の一生が過酷すぎる【写真あり】| 江戸ガイド ("Also Infected with Syphilis").
[9] Weber, Zoe. "From Courtesan to Geisha by Zoe Weber." ON EAST, 2014, https://oneast.sa.utoronto.ca/publication/2013-14/essays/from_courtesan_to_geisha/.

Japan also has a comparably extensive history involving indentured labor. A significant slave trade had existed since the Portuguese arrived in the 16th century. During this time, Japanese women were either purchased or abducted and transported back to Portugal to serve as sex slaves. A number of these women were retained as concubines by the crewmembers of the vessels engaged in trade with Japan.[10]

The Tokugawa shogunate's decision to legalize prostitution and confine sex work by women and girls to specific areas was primarily driven by the objective of streamlining tax collection, rather than moral concerns. A tax was levied on both the owners of the brothels and the prostitutes themselves. The presence of these quarters also contributed to the legitimization of prostitution, and the sale of women and girls for sexual purposes accelerated at an alarming rate.[11]

It is worth noting that not all prostitutes were coerced into sex work; some did so voluntarily, typically for financial reasons. While alternative routes to economic independence and social advancement for women existed throughout the Edo period, prostitution remained an ever-present source of income for women of all social classes. As a result, the female body evolved into a practical commodity that benefitted a broad spectrum of individuals in Japanese society.[12]

However, while males were preoccupied with indulging in pleasure-seeking activities and forgetting the difficulties arising from living in a

---

[10] Ohkubo, Kristine. *Nickname Flower of* Evil (呼び名は悪の花): The Abe Sada Story. 2019. Page 2.
[11] Lublin, Elizabeth D. "Sex Work During the Tokugawa Era." Oxford Research Encyclopedia of Asian History, 15 Sept. 2022, https://oxfordre.com/asianhistory/display/10.1093/acrefore/9780190277727.001.0001/acrefore-9780190277727-e-
[12] Weber, Zoe. "From Courtesan to Geisha by Zoe Weber."

highly regulated social structure, the emotions and thoughts of the women remain unknown to us. No true records of the Edo period prostitutes' personal thoughts and experiences exist, so we do not have their firsthand accounts. Art, literature, and certain historical accounts authored by men romanticize the pleasure quarters, but when viewed through the lens of a woman, it must have been an extremely miserable existence.[13]

---

[13] Hix, Lisa. "Sex and Suffering: The Tragic Life of the Japanese Courtesan." Ms. Magazine, 19 July 2018, msmagazine.com/2015/03/27/sex-and-suffering-the-tragic-life-of-the-japanese-courtesan/.

Sex and Marriage in Premodern Japan

Marriage, as it is currently understood, did not exist in the early history of Japan. Arranged marriages and polygamy were common during the Heian period (794-1185), a time marked by intellectual and cultural advancements and the rise of the samurai class. Both men and women engaged in extramarital relationships and openly pursued romantic partners during this era. The women participated in these liaisons without feeling remorse, and society held worldly women in high regard.

While it was customary for aristocratic men to maintain numerous wives concurrently, aristocratic women were restricted to having one husband at any given time.[14] In lieu of a formal wedding ceremony, the father of the bride and her intended partner reached a private agreement regarding the specifics of the union. Following the wedding, the wife resided separately from her husband and assumed responsibility for the upbringing of any heirs that were produced from their union.[15] Marriage was intended to produce offspring who would succeed to the highest possible rank in Heian society, which was structured according to a complex ranking system.[16] Both spouses were permitted to remarry following a divorce, which could be initiated by either spouse.[17] Lower-

---

[14] Aarsman, Mieke. "Omiai: Love and Sex in Ancient Japan." Tokiotours; Your Personal Tour Guide in Tokyo, 14 July 2013, tokiotours.wordpress.com/2013/07/14/omiai-love-and-sex-in-ancient-japan/.
[15] Kirwan, Christy. "Women in the Heian Court: Wives, Concubines, and Lovers." Owlcation, 18 Nov. 2023, owlcation.com/humanities/Women-in-the-Heian-Court.
[16] "Marriage in Japan." Wikiwand, www.wikiwand.com/en/Marriage_in_Japan. Accessed 12 May 2023.
[17] Kirwan, Christy. "Women in the Heian Court."

class men were financially constrained and could not support additional wives, but they were able to change spouses with ease.

Aristocratic daughters who were unable to secure marriages into suitable families had the option to become concubines for high-ranking noblemen and imperial family members. These women were obligated to develop specific proficiencies in poetry recitation, calligraphy, and music in order to progress in this fashion. By securing the support of a prominent patron, they had the potential to improve their social standing and that of their families.

Nonetheless, social ascent as a concubine was not without its challenges. These women were sometimes treated with contempt by their peers. Should an aristocratic gentleman exhibit an extreme preference for a certain concubine, that individual faced the peril of severe harassment at the hands of competing concubines.[18]

Throughout the Edo period, society was firmly stratified by the shogunate, which ranked individuals according to their social class at birth.[19] The *mibunsei* (identity system) was created to help bring stability to the country and consisted of the emperor, the court nobles, the shogun, and the *daimyo* (feudal lords) in the upper tier. Below them, the population was divided into *shinokosho* (four classes): the samurai, the farming peasants, the artisans, and the merchants.[20] Every family was required to register with their local authority and copies of these family registries were then sent to the shogunate. The social status of each individual was fixed in these registers. As a result, the main purpose of

---

[18] Kirwan, Christy. "Women in the Heian Court."
[19] Aarsman, Mieke. "Omiai: Love and Sex in Ancient Japan."
[20] Ohkubo, Kristine. *Nickname Flower of Evil*. Page 20.

marriage shifted from producing offspring to maintaining or improving the social status of the household. Families took great care to make sure their sons and daughters married to someone of equal or higher status.[21]

In a society where individuals pursued or were coerced into marriage for reasons other than love, the pleasure quarters assumed great significance. Men sought passion and love from prostitutes. Patrons of the pleasure quarters wanted to believe that their preferred courtesans were actually in love with them.[22]

---

[21] Aarsman, Mieke. "Omiai: Love and Sex in Ancient Japan."
[22] Hix, Lisa. "Sex and Suffering: The Tragic Life of the Japanese Courtesan."

iii. Illustration from "Complete Set of Fifty-four Chapters of the Tale of Genji"[23] by Ogata Gekkō, 1893. Public domain.

---

[23] The Tale of Genji is a classic work of Japanese literature written in the early 11th century by the noblewoman, poet, and lady-in-waiting Murasaki Shikibu. The original manuscript, created around the peak of the Heian period, no longer exists. The work is a unique depiction of the lifestyles of high courtiers during the Heian period.

"The role of miko has been present in Japan for many centuries and is rooted in the belief that young women have a special spiritual purity that allows them to serve the kami (gods) of the shrine. Miko are believed to be messengers between the human world and the divine realm."

—Irene Sue
"Miko: The Shrine Maiden"
May 10, 2023

iv. Aruki miko depicted on a six-panel folding screen from "Views in and around Kyoto" ("Rakuchu-Rakugai zu"), circa 1660. Artist unknown, public domain.

Aruki Miko

The term *miko* has multiple translations. The kanji for miko can be interpreted as a combination of "god" and "child" or as "shaman child" in archaic terms. Alternative terms for miko include *ichiko*, signifying "female medium" or "fortuneteller," and *reibai*, denoting "spirit go-between" or "spirit medium." Typically, however, the term miko is currently translated as "shrine maiden" or "female shaman" in the English language.[24]

Miko traditions originated during Japan's prehistoric Jomon period (circa 14,000-300 BCE), when female shamans entered trances and conveyed the divine messages of the *kami* (gods). The role of a shaman was traditionally inherited through generations, although there were instances where non-bloodline girls willingly received training or were chosen by local chieftains, which caused a disruption in the hereditary succession.

To attain the status of a shaman, the young lady, who was in the early stages of adolescence and had recently begun to menstruate, had to undergo an arduous and demanding training process. A respected and experienced elder female shaman, potentially a family member or a member of the tribe, would instruct the young girl in the necessary procedures to master going into a trance. She also studied to become a medium by learning to effectively communicate with kami and spirits of the deceased. Eventually, she acquired knowledge of a secret language exclusively understood by a select group of individuals, the other

---

[24] Writers, YABAI. "Miko: The Shrine Maidens of Japan," Yabai.com. http://yabai.com/p/2317.

shamans within the tribe, thus unveiling the mysteries of divination and incantations.

Following a training period that lasted from three to seven years, the girl completed an initiation ceremony and officially became a shaman. The secret ceremony was witnessed by her mentor, along with other respected elders and other shamans. Comparable to a matrimonial rite, the apprentice, who was a virgin at the time, underwent a metamorphosis to become the bride of the deity she devoted herself to. A long-defunct custom dictated that miko engage in sexual relations with a *kannushi,* who served as a representative of the kami. Thus, any child that resulted from the act would be regarded as the progeny of the kami.

During the Kamakura period (1192 to 1333), many miko were left without financial support when the temples and shrines that used to sustain them went bankrupt. As a result, some of the shrine maidens started to wander in search of a new means of subsistence. They were called *aruki miko*, which means walking miko. Although the main function of the aruki miko was to perform religious/shamanistic rituals, they were commonly linked to prostitution. In fact, sexual activity is not considered a taboo within the Shinto faith.[25]

Early miko held a high social position and had strong connections to the governing class. In addition to their ceremonial duties, the miko fulfilled diverse roles in both religious and political contexts. With the emergence of the aruki miko, however, the miko's stature as women close to the kami diminished.[26]

---

[25] "Prostitution in Japan." Wikipedia.
[26] "Miko." Wikipedia, Wikimedia Foundation, 24 Oct. 2023, en.wikipedia.org/wiki/Miko.

As the social importance of spirit medium functions decreased and fewer shrines and temples could afford to employ them, the shrine maidens had to find other ways to financially sustain themselves. Consequently, they became part of a group of entertainers that provided both amusement and sexual services to visitors who arrived at the various *shuku* along the *Tokaido*.[27]

The *Tokaido* (Eastern Sea Road) was part of the Five Routes, a network of roadways established by Tokugawa Ieyasu, the first Shogun of Japan, to connect Edo with the rest of the country. The *Tokaido* connected Edo with the city of Kyoto. There were 53 post stations, referred to as *shuku*, along this road. These stations offered stables, food, and accommodations to travelers, and ensured a steady stream of clients for the miko.[28]

These days, the miko are mostly involved in the daily operations of larger shrines, including maintaining the grounds, performing office tasks, and working in the shrine's shop. They assist the priests in ceremonial and ritual contexts.

---

[27] Kuly, Lisa. "Locating Transcendence in Japanese Minzoku Geinô: Yamabushi and Miko Kagura – Ethnologies." Érudit, Association Canadienne d'Ethnologie et de Folklore, 20 Oct. 2003, www.erudit.org/en/journals/ethno/2003-v25-n1-ethno557/007130ar/.
[28] "The Fifty-Three Stations of the Tōkaidō." Wikipedia, Wikimedia Foundation, 27 Aug. 2023, en.wikipedia.org/wiki/The_Fifty-three_Stations_of_the_T%C5%8Dkaid%C5%8D.

v. *Izumo no Okuni, by an anonymous artist from the school of Matabei Kan'ei Era (1624-1644). Part of a six-panel screen, public domain.*

Izumo no Okuni

Izumo no Okuni, who lived around 1578-1613, was undoubtedly one of the most famous of the shrine maidens. In addition to being a miko, she was a prostitute, a performer, and the celebrated inventor of *kabuki*.

Kabuki, a long-established form of Japanese theater, combines traditional dance with dramatic performance. Kabuki theatre is renowned for its intricate *kumadori*[29] makeup, extravagant and ornate costumes, and stylized theatrical performances.[30]

Okuni was born around 1578 in the vicinity of the Izumo shrine, where several members of her family served and where her father, Nakamura Sanemon, was employed as a blacksmith. Eventually, Okuni became a miko, a position in which she gained recognition for her beauty and for her dancing and dramatic skills. Due to the prevailing tradition, priests, miko, and other individuals were often sent to solicit funds for the shrine. Okuni was thus sent to Kyoto to showcase her sacred dances and songs in order to earn money.

Her fame for performing the *nembutsu odori* (nembutsu dance) grew during her stay in Kyoto. Although this dance may be traced back to Kuya, a 10th-century apostle of Pure Land Buddhism, by the time Okuni popularized it, it had largely evolved into a secular folk dance. Her specific rendition was recognized for its seductiveness and suggestive undertones. Okuni's performances also featured comedic sketches

---

[29] In general, Kumadori makeup comprises vibrantly hued stripes or patterns applied atop a foundation of white, with each hue and pattern representing a distinct facet of the character.
[30] "Kabuki." Wikipedia, Wikimedia Foundation, 12 Nov. 2023, en.wikipedia.org/wiki/Kabuki.

depicting romantic encounters in different public venues and interactions between men and prostitutes. Amidst these and various other dances and performances, she attracted significant attention and began to draw large crowds wherever she performed. Ultimately, she was called to return to the Izumo shrine, but she chose to disregard the summons and sent money instead.

Okuni established a new dance theater style in 1603, featuring a group of female performers on an improvised stage built on the dry riverbed of the Kamo River in Kyoto. She recruited socially disadvantaged women, especially those involved in prostitution, from the area and taught them singing, dancing, and acting to establish her troupe.

The performances put on by Okuni's troupe were commonly labeled "kabuki" due to their extraordinary style and brazenness. The word was derived from the term *kabukimono*, which was used to describe those who were oddly dressed and swaggering on the street.

Early kabuki performances consisted of aimless songs and dances, and were frequently criticized for being excessively erotic and cacophonous, but praised for their vibrancy and aesthetic appeal. Since the troupe led by Okuni consisted solely of women, she required that her actresses portray characters of both genders. As her troupe became well-known, she was imitated by numerous others, notably in brothels that provided similar performances to entertain rich patrons and recruit prostitutes with desirable acting and singing skills.[31]

---

[31] "Izumo No Okuni." Wikipedia, Wikimedia Foundation, en.wikipedia.org/wiki/Izumo_no_Okuni.

The popularity of kabuki during this period was largely attributed to the risqué and suggestive themes presented by numerous ensembles. The appeal of kabuki was further enhanced by the fact that its main actors also engaged in prostitution. For this reason, kabuki was alternatively labeled "prostitute kabuki" throughout this time period.[32]

Okuni ended her professional activities in 1610 and subsequently vanished from the public eye. In 1629, shogun Tokugawa Iemitsu prohibited women from participating in kabuki due to public demand for moral reform and concern over conflicts arising from men's competitions for actresses' affections. Young men swiftly took over the roles of actors and "actresses," but this practice was soon prohibited too due to concerns about male prostitution and moral corruption. As a result, performances were limited to older males, a tradition that continues at official kabuki theaters to this day.[33]

---

[32] "Kabuki." Wikipedia.
[33] "Izumo No Okuni." Wikipedia.

vi. Izumo no Okuni on stage, as depicted in the illustrated manuscript KUNIJO KABUKI EKOTOBA (Kuni's Kabuki). Public domain.

"The younger women melt men's hearts with rouge and powder and songs and smiles ... Ah! ... a tryst in a boat on the waves equals a lifetime of delightful encounters."

Oe Yukitoki (955-1010), courtier-poet

vii. Fragment of the "Illustrated Life of Priest Honen," 13th to early 14th century. This depicts an asobi trio in their boat approaching the priest sent to exile in Tosa. Public domain.

The Asobi

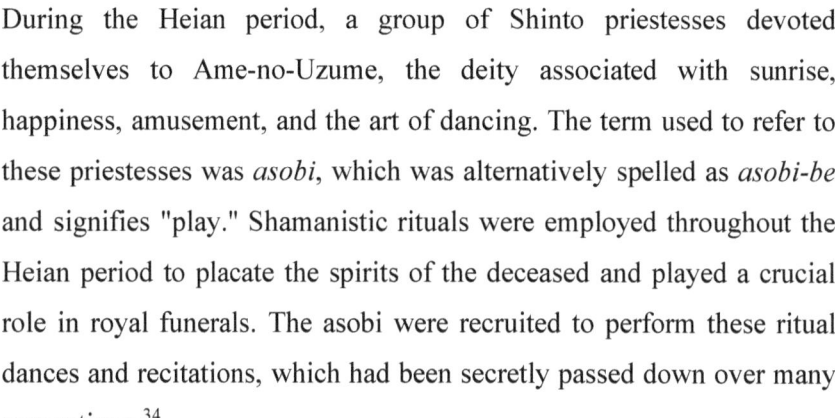

During the Heian period, a group of Shinto priestesses devoted themselves to Ame-no-Uzume, the deity associated with sunrise, happiness, amusement, and the art of dancing. The term used to refer to these priestesses was *asobi*, which was alternatively spelled as *asobi-be* and signifies "play." Shamanistic rituals were employed throughout the Heian period to placate the spirits of the deceased and played a crucial role in royal funerals. The asobi were recruited to perform these ritual dances and recitations, which had been secretly passed down over many generations.[34]

Buddhism spurred a decline in the asobi's participation at royal funerals; in its place, they became recognized for their *imayo* melodies. The earthy and flirtatious style of these folk songs made them immensely popular at the Heian court.[35] The asobi managed to maintain their livelihoods by performing these songs and by engaging in sexual acts in return for gifts. Although their profession exhibited characteristics akin to those of prostitutes, they were considered entertainers due to their musical ability.[36]

The asobi also utilized a unique naming convention. They transitioned from the naming practices of the Heian period, which relied on identifying individuals according to their lineage, rank, social status, or

---

[34] "Asobi (Ancient Japan)." Wikipedia, en.wikipedia.org/wiki/Asobi_(ancient_Japan).
[35] Yu, A. C. "Imayo (A Popular Style of Japanese Songs in the Heian Period) - Japanese Wiki Corpus." Imayo (a Popular Style of Japanese Songs in the Heian Period) - Japanese Wiki Corpus, www.japanesewiki.com/culture/Imayo%20(a%20popular%20style%20of%20Japanese%20songs%20in%20the%20Heian%20period).html. Accessed 10 July 2023.
[36] "Asobi (Ancient Japan)." Wikipedia.

role within the court, to adopting personalized names for each individual. The use of this naming convention, which resembled a stage name, indicated that the asobi had a higher social position that extended beyond the boundaries of their patriarchal families and court hierarchy.[37]

After the introduction of the *Taiho Reform Code* in 701 CE and the *Yoro Code* in 718 CE, the overall perception of the asobi changed, and they were regarded as immoral individuals. The adoption of these rules, which replicated the administrative and legal systems of China, aimed to consolidate the government's authority. Due to the significant impact of Confucianism on China's government, Japan also adopted the Confucian value of diligence, with a specific focus on enhancing agricultural output. Asobi, being exempt from compulsory labor, did not contribute to agricultural activities and were considered unproductive.[38]

Due to the increasing impact of Buddhism and the implementation of the Taiho reforms, the revered status of the asobi diminished. The mostly male Buddhist clergy took over the handling of royal funeral activities, while the asobi, who were formerly at the heart of the religious domain, underwent a growing marginalization in society.[39]

During the late 11th century, the asobi began establishing permanent towns along the rivers that were commonly used by pilgrims and tourists. The most notable asobi communities included the Eguchi settlement located along the Yodo River, as well as the Kanzaki and Kanishima

---

[37] Asobi (Ancient Japan)." Wikipedia.
[38] Asobi (Ancient Japan)." Wikipedia.
[39] Asobi (Ancient Japan)." Wikipedia.

settlements situated near the Kanzaki River. The two rivers functioned as the primary transportation route from the inland sea to the capital.[40]

With the growth of trade at the river ports, the popularity of asobi performances increased. Furthermore, there were many shrines alongside the river which attracted a large influx of pilgrims. A considerable number of these pilgrims patronized the asobi. Although the asobi would occasionally visit their clients' residences, patrons often sought entertainment at the shuku or *yado*, which are inns situated along highways. Thus, the asobi were able to attain land ownership, a status that was exclusively reserved for the most affluent members of Heian society, due to their remarkable achievements as entertainers.[41]

The asobi's organizational hierarchy was overseen by a female leader referred to as a *choja* or *mune*. These women achieved their leadership status as a result of their exceptional personal charisma and excellent imayo talents. Moreover, their selection may have been swayed by their personal connections and wealth, as certain asobi women originated from influential families that had experienced a decline in their positions of power. The position of choja was commonly passed down from mothers to daughters. The primary responsibilities of these leaders were to protect

---

[40] Kim, Yung-Hee. *Songs to Make the Dust Dance: The Ryojin Hisho of Twelfth-Century Japan.* University of California Press, 1994. publishing.cdlib.org/ucpressebooks/view?docId=ft2f59n7x0&chunk.id=d0e769&toc.id=d0e769&brand=ucpress.
[41] "Asobi (Ancient Japan)." Wikipedia.

the group members from unscrupulous clients, maintain group cohesion, and distribute resources as needed among the members.[42]

Asobi also conducted business on the water, using their boats to attract potential clients. After their clientele boarded the vessel, the asobi captivated them through imayo singing and rendered sexual favors. One principal asobi was responsible for singing and beating a small drum; one apprentice asobi was tasked with tending to her mistress and carrying a large parasol; and one elderly asobi was entrusted with rowing the vessel. This comprised the minimum number of crew members for an average asobi boat. Given their reputation as accomplished performers, the asobi were permitted to overtly solicit customers in broad daylight in the presence of onlookers. Asobi often formed marital alliances with aristocratic families due to their remarkable intelligence and charisma, which attracted the highest-ranking nobles.[43]

The asobi, in their post-Buddhist capacities, continued to embody certain shamanistic attributes while functioning as entertainers. Consequently, engaging in sexual activity with an asobi was considered a sacred practice.[44]

To ensure their economic well-being, the asobi initiated a ritualistic observance of the deity Hyakudayu. Hyakudayu worship is a religious practice centered around the reverence of phallic symbols made from materials such as stone, paper, or wood. Oe no Masafusa, a renowned poet, scholar, and tutor who lived from 1041 to 1111, wrote about these women in his historical book, *Yujoki*. In it, he explains how the asobi had

---

[42] "Asobi (Ancient Japan)." Wikipedia.
[43] Kim, Yung-Hee. Songs to Make the Dust Dance.
[44] Asobi (Ancient Japan)." Wikipedia.

thousands of phallic objects. It was believed that praying to these objects and honoring Hyakudayu ensured continued success in attracting male customers.

The Hirota Shrine and the Sumiyoshi Shrine, known for their Hyakudayu rituals, were popular destinations for the asobi to visit during their pilgrimages. The aristocracy's strong fondness for these shrines created opportunities for the asobi to engage with them.[45]

In contrast to the Edo period courtesans, texts exist that incorporate the asobi's personal viewpoints. Otamae, a 70-year-old asobi, was called to court by emperor Go-Shirakawa during the twelfth century. She taught the emperor the imayo style of her family and dedicated the following fourteen years to sharing her repertoire with him.

A portion of these melodies remain since the emperor inscribed them into the *Ryojin Hisho* document. This compilation of imayo melodies presents an assortment of viewpoints expressed by the asobi women. While some songs candidly extol the gratifications of sexual activity, others offer a more realistic portrayal of the asobi's lives. A limited number of affluent men chose asobi as concubines or spouses, and some women expressed their disillusionment in songs when the men they had eagerly expected to wed abandoned them for someone else. As opposed to the comparatively refined court poems of that era, which seldom address the subject of parental love, asobi sang frequently of their affection for their children, and bemoaned the fact that their daughters had followed in their footsteps

---

[45] "Asobi (Ancient Japan)." Wikipedia.

and entered the sex trade or decried the affluent members of society who sold the asobi's sons into servitude.[46]

Asobi are occasionally mistaken for *kugutsume*. Although the two types of women have certain similarities, they are not the same. *Kugutsume* were part of a traveling group of *kugutsushi* (puppeteers) that included both sexes. While both genders staged puppet shows to *kugutsu mawashi* music, the women indulged in prostitution and the males in sword dancing.[47] In contrast to the asobi, who solicited customers along the river, the *kugutsume* women practiced mostly on the interior footpaths in Aohaka, Sunomata, and Nogami.[48]

A third group of women existed during the late Heian period; they performed a distinctive sword dance while singing imayo songs. These women were designated as *shirabyoshi* and were attired in male clothing.

The shirabyoshi quickly gained the favor of aristocratic men and grew in popularity. Emperor Go-Toba, the 82nd emperor of Japan, was the most renowned patron of the shirabyoshi. He invited a large number of women on excursions and selected several of them as concubines. Thus, the shirabyoshi achieved a level of popularity that surpassed that of the asobi.[49]

---

[46] Hyland, Meg. "Kokannon." Women of 1000 AD, womenof1000ad.weebly.com/kokannon.html.
[47] Yu, A. C. "Tekiya," Japanese Wiki Corpus www.japanesewiki.com/culture/Tekiya.html. Accessed 21 Feb. 2024.
[48] "Asobi (Ancient Japan)." Wikipedia.
[49] "Asobi (Ancient Japan)." Wikipedia.

"Kugutsu are folk without anywhere to call a home, and erect their tents at will under the heavens, as water and fodder demand—much in the manner of the horse-peoples [of North China]. Kugutsu men are masters of the horse-bow and some among them juggle swords, or many balls, and even fight wrestling bouts with fine peach-wood puppets.

Kugutsu girls paint their eyes, in order to appear dour and somber. Yet, they swing their hips as they walk, and shockingly bare their teeth when they smile, even using red powders on their cheeks for effect. Their actions hint at sexual pleasure, and they use their charms to lure young men to their arms."

— *Kuiraishi-no-ki* by Oe no Masafusa, circa 1070

viii. Shizuka Gozen by Katsushika Hokusai, circa 1825. Public domain.

The Shirabyoshi

As previously mentioned, the shirabyoshi were female performers who provided entertainment to audiences in Japan throughout the Heian and Kamakura periods. They were known for their singing and dancing abilities, wore masculine attire, and entertained the nobility, in addition to engaging in celebrations.

The standard attire of the shirabyoshi comprised a *tate-eboshi*, a tall black hat worn at court, a *tachi*, a long, single-edged samurai sword slung from the waist, *hakama*, which were pants resembling skirts, and *suikan*, a type of jacket. Red or white in color, the *suikan* was a single-breasted jacket featuring open sides and a collar fastened with a *kumihimo* (a traditional braided silk cord).

Shirabyoshi also used *oshiroi*, a type of white facial makeup. It covered their faces and necks, and their eyebrows were painted higher on their foreheads (*hikimayu*). Their hair was styled in a simple way, left at a considerable length and gathered into a relaxed ponytail fastened with a ribbon, known as a *takenaga*.

The shirabyoshi engaged in sexual relationships with their patrons and bore children of noble lineage; however, it is important to note that, unlike the asobi, this was not their primary role as entertainers.

Like the asobi, the shirabyoshi also engaged in the performance of imayo melodies by singing and dancing. The word shirabyoshi is thought to perhaps mean "simple rhythm," which refers to the rhythmic pattern of the imayo.

The shirabyoshi emerged midway through the Heian period. A number of aristocratic families experienced unfortunate reversals of their fortunes as a result of societal transformation and the transfer of power that occurred during this time period. In order to guarantee their families' survival, the daughters of these families were compelled to perform as shirabyoshi. These girls, who were educated and cultivated, evolved into an elite group of courtesans distinguished by their intellectual prowess and their artistic abilities, singing, dancing, and poetic talents. As a result of their prominence as entertainers during the 12th century, a considerable number of women aspired to become shirabyoshi. However, their popularity began to wane in the 13th century and they vanished from society in the 14th century.[50]

One of the most renowned figures in Japanese history and literature, Shizuka Gozen, also known as Lady Shizuka, was a shirabyoshi. She was the mistress of Minamoto no Yoshitsune, a military commander of the Minamoto clan during the late Heian and early Kamakura periods. His older half-brother, Minamoto no Yoritomo, established the Kamakura shogunate.

The Iso area in Aminocho town in the old Tango Province (modern-day northern Kyoto Prefecture) is commonly believed to have been Shizuka's birthplace. Iso no Zenji, her mother, was also a shirabyoshi. According to legend, Emperor Go-Shirakawa invited Shizuka and ninety-nine other dancers to pray for rain during a severe and prolonged drought. While the ninety-nine dancers were unable to induce rain, the arrival of Shizuka

---

[50] "Shirabyōshi." Wikipedia, Wikimedia Foundation, en.wikipedia.org/wiki/Shiraby%C5%8Dshi.

produced the desired outcome. The emperor subsequently praised her, and it was during this time that she met Yoshitsune.[51]

In 1185, Yoshitsune fled from Kyoto after joining forces with his uncle, Minamoto no Yukiie, to oppose Yoritomo. He brought twelve women with whom he maintained intimate relationships and his warriors. But he soon realized that this enormous retinue was slowing him down and sent all the women back, including his favorite, Shizuka, who was pregnant with his child.

Upon her arrival in Kyoto, she was apprehended and escorted to Yoritomo's court. She was questioned about the whereabouts of Yoshitsune, but she remained silent and did not disclose any information. Later, a significantly more severe situation unfolded. Upon learning of her pregnancy, the merciless Yoritomo commanded that if the child happened to be a male, he must be executed, as he could not afford to let any of Yoshitsune's sons survive.[52] Shizuka gave birth to a son, who was promptly slain by his uncle Yoritomo.[53]

Prior to setting Shizuka free, Yoritomo was determined to see the performance of this highly renowned dancer. He issued an order for her to perform a dance in his presence. She refused. Afterward, his followers convinced her to take part in a supplication dance before the deities at Hachiman Shrine. She acquiesced and performed the dance, but quickly understood that she had been deceived. Yoritomo had observed her

---

[51] "Shizuka Gozen." Wikipedia, Wikimedia Foundation, 12 Jan. 2023, en.wikipedia.org/wiki/Shizuka_Gozen.
[52] Downer, Lesley. "Women of the Pleasure Quarters: The Secret History of the Geisha." The New York Times, 13 May 2001, archive.nytimes.com/www.nytimes.com/books/first/d/downer-01pleasure.html.
[53] "Shizuka Gozen." Wikipedia.

performance discreetly from a concealed position behind a bamboo blind. Upon realizing this, she burst into a fervent love song. With great passion, she expressed her adoration for Yoshitsune, her intense longing for him, and her elation that he had skillfully eluded his malevolent half-brother Yoritomo. Yoritomo experienced conflicting emotions of anger towards the audacity she displayed and delight in the exceptional beauty of her voice. However, as she was just a woman, he considered her to be harmless and hence chose not to punish her.

There are conflicting accounts of what transpired following Shizuka's release. According to some accounts, she cut her floor-length hair, shaved her head and became a nun. A year later, at the age of 19, she succumbed to grief and died.[54]

Today, you can find several tombs associated with her. They are situated on Awaji Island, in Kurihashi Town, Kitakatsushika-gun, Saitama Prefecture, and in the former Tochio City, Niigata Prefecture. Shizuka is a key character in the Noh play *Funa Benkei* and the bunraku play *Yoshitsune Senbon Zakura*. These plays were eventually adapted to kabuki. She also appears in several other traditional and modern works of literature and drama.

---

[54] Downer, Lesley. Women of the Pleasure Quarters: The Secret History of the Geisha.

"A tale of prostitution is undoubtedly a larger commentary on women's place in Japan and their struggle to survive in a society that places a high value on their sexuality and a low value on their humanity."

—Aidan Djabarov, Writer
"COURTESANS & CASH"
December 21, 2018

ix. Second-Floor Parlor in New Yoshiwara by Okumura Masanobu, circa 1745. Public domain.

Prostitution During the Edo Period

The Tokugawa Shogunate is credited with founding the immensely popular Yoshiwara pleasure quarter in Edo in 1617. However, the first red-light district in Japan was established in Kyoto in 1589, during the reign of Toyotomi Hideyoshi, Tokugawa's predecessor. Hara Saburoemon, a stable hand under Hideyoshi's command, formally petitioned the warlord for authorization to establish a brothel. His request was duly granted. Near the imperial palace, he built a small, walled area featuring a single gate. It was given the name *Yanagimachi*, which means "Willow Town." To attract the affluent and sophisticated gentlemen of Kyoto, he established brothels and teahouses staffed with educated, high-class courtesans.[55]

Yanagimachi achieved instantaneous success. Even Hideyoshi and his retainers occasionally visited the pleasure quarter in disguise. Nevertheless, the proximity of the red-light district to the emperor's residence necessitated its relocation. In 1602, it was reestablished in the south-central region of the city as *Rokujo-Misujimachi*. The shogunate eventually issued another directive to relocate it to a more secluded location west of the Nishi Honganji temple. Constructed in 1641, *Shimabara* was surrounded by a moat and a tall wall, which included a spectacular entrance located in the east end. From the outside, Shimabara resembled a fortress rather than a red-light district.[56]

---

[55] Downer, Lesley. Women of the Pleasure Quarters: The Secret History of the Geisha.
[56] Choi, Eunice. "Kyoto: Pleasure Quarters." Kyoto: Architecture 1562-1657, www.columbia.edu/itc/ealac/V3613/kyoto/recreational/pleasure.html. Accessed 25 Sept. 2023.

Under the administration of the Tokugawa shogunate, Japan enjoyed a period of peace, economic growth, and cultural development. Driven by a desire to benefit from the growing abundance of riches, people relocated to the rapidly expanding urban areas.[57] Although the merchants amassed great fortunes, they were strictly forbidden from using them to enhance their social status, regardless of their level of prosperity. Moreover, as their wealth increased, the probability of the government confiscating everything they owned also escalated.

Merchants were exempted from paying taxes because of the benefits and privileges it would have provided them. Despite this, the shogunate occasionally found an excuse to seize their funds. Therefore, it appeared rational to expeditiously, and without discrimination, dispose of one's wealth. The thriving pleasure quarters provided an ideal environment for the successful execution of this plan.

The pleasure quarters swiftly transformed into the most lavish district of the city. Even the imperial nobles and samurai stole away for clandestine visits. The pleasure quarters provided everything a refined gentleman could desire—sophisticated conversations with beautiful women, culture, sex, and romance. It also served as a venue for merchants to host their clientele and display their wealth.

In 1661, a writer named Asai Ryoi used the term *ukiyo* (the floating world) to describe this unique lifestyle. From this word came the term *ukiyo-e* (illustrations of the floating world). Ukiyo-e pertains to the woodblock prints that portray the denizens of the era, namely courtesans,

---

[57] "Edo Period." Wikipedia, Wikimedia Foundation, 21 Sept. 2023, en.wikipedia.org/wiki/Edo period.

prostitutes, and subsequently geisha. Initially, the term "ukiyo" originated in Buddhism and denoted the transient nature of everything.

Indeed, the pleasure quarter was an ephemeral world where the men could escape from their work and family waiting outside its gates. It was said that when men visited the pleasure quarters, they would forget what time of day it was, what period of history it was, and they even forgot about their wives.

Every pleasure district cultivated its own dialect, which was an endearingly courteous yet whimsically alluring slang. Thus, any woman who successfully escaped the pleasure quarter where she was enslaved could be recognized, based on her manner of speech, and sent back.

To the men, the pleasure quarters appeared as if they were in an exotic foreign land or a dream world. This was not the case for the women. They both lived and worked there. They were powerless to leave, even if they wanted to. Despite their opulence and allure, they were essentially slaves of the brothel proprietors.

The brothel proprietor was the rightful owner of the girls and women. Prior to their arrival, they had already accrued a substantial debt due to the expenses associated with purchasing them from their parents. The brothel furnished them with meals and kimonos; however, the cost of each grain of rice and bolt of silk merely contributed to their growing debts. When they reached the legal age to begin working, their debt had escalated to such a level that they were compelled to engage in continuous work in order to repay it.

The one chance of escape—if a woman wanted it—was to find someone prepared to buy out her contract and make her his wife or mistress.[58]

Prostitution was a flourishing industry during the Edo period. By the first half of the 17th century, there were three main pleasure quarters operating near the outskirts of Japan's three major cities: **Shinmachi** in Osaka, **Shimabara** in Kyoto, and **Yoshiwara** in Edo. In 1642, the Maruyama pleasure quarter was established in Nagasaki, and it became the only red-light district to cater to foreigners. Only the prostitutes from Maruyama were permitted to service the Chinese in Nagasaki and the Dutch in Dejima. While seldom discussed, the Furuichi pleasure quarter in Ise was equally well-known for serving the Japanese religious pilgrims who came to visit the Ise Grand Shrine. Furthermore, throughout the nation, there were more than twenty less-known licensed red-light districts and a multitude of illicit private brothels.

The prostitutes of Maruyama were divided into two distinct categories. Those who serviced the Chinese were called *karayuki-san* (literally, "Miss Gone-to-China").[59] During the second half of the 19th century, the word evolved to mean "Miss Gone Abroad" and was used to describe the Japanese women who travelled to, or were trafficked, to various parts of the Asia-Pacific region to work as prostitutes, courtesans, and geisha. Those who serviced the Dutch were called *orandayuki-san*.[60]

With the gradual enforcement of the Japan's policy of seclusion from the outside world, trade relations with the country were limited to the Chinese

---

[58] Downer, Lesley. Women of the Pleasure Quarters: The Secret History of the Geisha.
[59] "遊女 (Yujo)." Wikipedia, Wikimedia Foundation, 15 Aug. 2023, ja.wikipedia.org/wiki/%E9%81%8A%E5%A5%B3.
[60] "Karayuki-San." Wikipedia, Wikimedia Foundation, 20 July 2023, en.wikipedia.org/wiki/Karayuki-san.

and the Dutch. The Dutch were restricted to Dejima, an artificial islet in the shape of a fan that had been formed through the excavation of a canal across a peninsula that extended into the Bay of Nagasaki. Women, with the exception of prostitutes, were forbidden to enter the islet and Dutchmen were prevented from going outside Dejima without permission.

When Nagasaki began flourishing as a commercial hub between 1592 and 1596, a large number of freelance prostitutes from the port city of Hakata arrived and dispersed throughout Nagasaki. These women were rounded up in 1642 and subsequently tasked with working in either Yoriai-machi or Maruyama-machi, collectively referred to as **Maruyama**. Maruyama was an amalgamation of two sub-wards.

Maruyama experienced a concurrent rise in prosperity as Japan's trade with mainland China and the Netherlands increased. During the period from 1673 to 1681, Maruyama was home to 54 brothels and 776 prostitutes. From that number, 127 women serviced the Japanese. Those who only catered to the Japanese were of the highest rank, similar to the *tayu* (the highest class of traditional courtesan in Japan) in Yoshiwara. They were selected on the basis of their appearance and their expertise in floral arrangement and the tea ceremony. Additionally, they possessed exceptional abilities in reading, writing, singing, and dancing. The ones who catered to the Dutch belonged to the lowest echelons of the profession. They resided beyond the pleasure quarter and were obligated to regularly register themselves as prostitutes. They were commonly known as the "name prostitutes."

At the end of the Edo period, as a result of declining business, there were 28 brothels with only 487 girls remaining in Maruyama.[61]

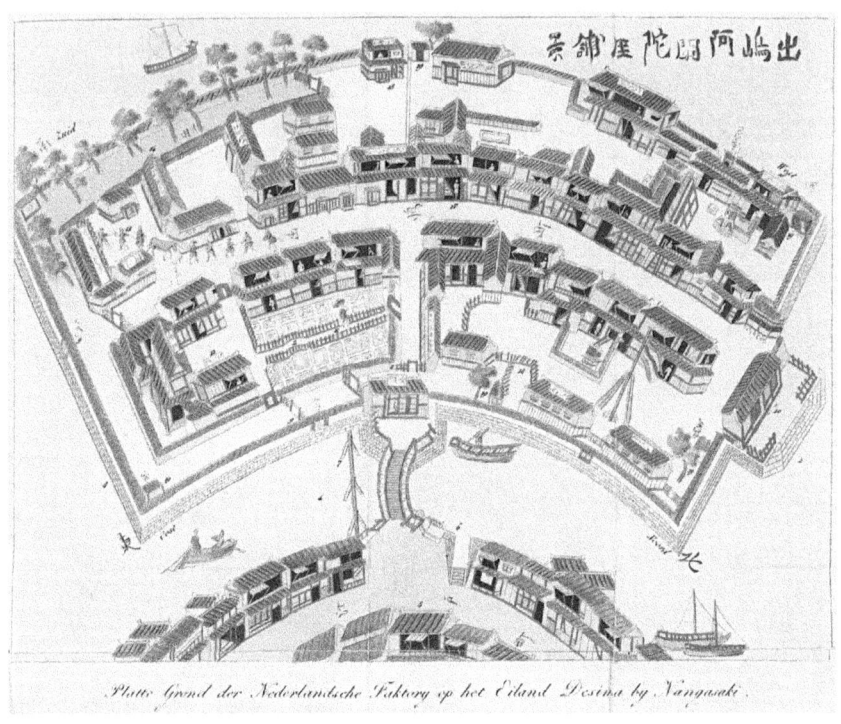

x. Ground-plan of the Dutch trade-post on the island Dejima at Nagasaki by Isaac Titsingh, circa 1824-1825. Public domain.

---

[61] "Forgotten Foibles: Love and the Dutch at Dejima (1641–1854)." Forgotten Foibles: Love and the Dutch at Dejima (1641–1854) | East Asian History, 2021, www.eastasianhistory.org/39/vos-foibles/index.html.

*"Only through the Great Gate
the courtesans
peep at the world."*

*— Reginald Horace Blyth
Japanese Life and Character in Senryu, 1961*

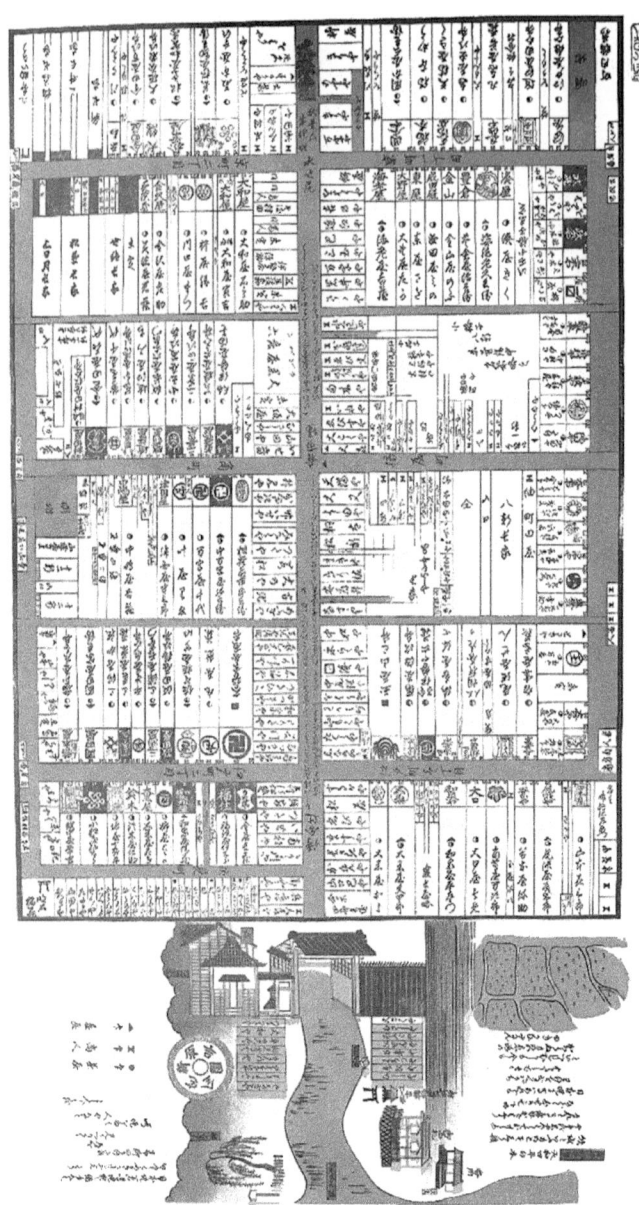

xi. Map of Yoshiwara, 1846. Public domain.

Yoshiwara: Tokyo's Red-Light District

xii. Mikaeri Yanagi by Utagawa Hiroshige, circa 1853. Public domain.

From 1660 to 1720, Japan's population increased twofold, and grew from 15 million to 30 million. The population rise led to increased urbanization and the growth and development of Japan's three major cities, Kyoto, Osaka, and Edo.[62] Within these urban areas, there was a significant disparity in the gender ratio with a surplus of men compared to women.

---

[62] Squires, Graham. "Edo Period." World History Encyclopedia, 11 Oct. 2022, www.worldhistory.org/Edo_Period/.

Consequently, the shogunate swiftly established officially sanctioned pleasure quarters in Kyoto, Osaka, and Edo.[63]

Yoshiwara was located in present-day Taito-ku, Senzoku 4-chome.[64] During its height, it was a vibrant district that garnered recognition both domestically and internationally, where noblemen and commoners were entertained by courtesans. Initially founded in 1617 on the outskirts of present-day *Ningyocho* (literally Doll Town), Yoshiwara was completely consumed by fire in 1657. This catastrophic incident, which later became known as the *Great Fire of Meireki*, destroyed the entire community. The red-light district was subsequently relocated to a marshland located to the north of present-day Asakusa. The marsh was drained and *Shin-Yoshiwara* or New Yoshiwara emerged. Eventually, the "New" was dropped from the name and people simply referred to the area as Yoshiwara.

In an effort to keep children and the criminal element out, Yoshiwara was walled in and enclosed by a moat. Its appearance as an island from the exterior gave rise to its nickname "the floating world."[65] Visitors entered and exited the district by a meandering path that was marked by a traditional Japanese torii gate, commonly found at the entrance of a Shinto shrine. In the same way that the torii signifies the shift from the ordinary to the sacred in a shrine setting, the Yoshiwara gate represented

---

[63] Kobayashi, Akira. "The Courtesans of Yoshiwara." Nippon.com, www.nippon.com/en/japan-topics/g01083/.
[64] Lloyd, George. "What Became of Yoshiwara, Tokyo's Old Red-Light District?" Japan Today, 23 June 2020, japantoday.com/category/features/travel/what-became-of-yoshiwara-tokyo%E2%80%99s-old-red-light-district.
[65] Sugoii Japan. "Yoshiwara - Discover the Old Tokyo Red Light District of Edo Period." Sugoii Japan, sugoii-japan.com/yoshiwara-tokyo-old-red-light-district.

the transition from the ties that maintained the social hierarchy of Edo to the new hierarchy of aesthetic, sensual, and sexual pleasure.

A willow tree was situated in close proximity to the entrance of Yoshiwara. It was referred to as the *mikaeri yanagi* or the backward glance willow. The designation originates from the practice of visitors to Yoshiwara who upon reaching the tree, cast a wistful look back before heading home.[66]

Customarily, transactions were conducted in nearby teahouses, outside the walled-in district and patrons were required to surrender their swords before they could enter. In order to arrange a meeting with the *oiran*, one was required to contact a go-between. This person was called a *yarite*.[67] Although the policy stipulated that visitors could only remain for a single night; this stipulation was never enforced. Some patrons loitered for days in the pleasure quarter.[68]

More than 9,000 women were employed in Yoshiwara by 1893. The majority of them spent their entire lives as *shinzo* (lower-ranking prostitutes), displayed to patrons in the *harimise* (a lattice-fronted room on the first floor of the brothel) awaiting selection. Only the Nakanocho (main street) in Yoshiwara was lined with harimise.[69]

While the social status of the patrons was inconsequential beyond the walls of Yoshiwara, a rigorous hierarchical structure was observed among

---

[66] Lloyd, George. "What Became of Yoshiwara, Tokyo's Old Red-Light District?"
[67] Iles, Stuart. "The Throw Away Temple – Dumping Ground of the Yoshiwara Prostitutes." Japanese History and Culture: Educational Studies of Japanese History, 5 Feb. 2015, rekishinihon.com/2015/02/06/the-throw-away-temple-dumping-ground-of-the-yoshiwara-prostitutes/.
[68] Sugoii Japan. "Yoshiwara - Discover the Old Tokyo Red Light District of Edo Period."
[69] "Yoshiwara." Wikipedia, 30 Apr. 2023, en.wikipedia.org/wiki/Yoshiwara.

the courtesans. The term "oiran" referred to the highest-ranked prostitutes, with stratified ranks in both the top and lower tiers. Of course, the higher-ranking prostitutes commanded a higher fee; therefore, the social hierarchy of clients mattered only with regard to how much money they could afford to spend.[70]

In 1913, Yoshiwara experienced another catastrophic fire that caused significant destruction, but it continued to operate nonetheless. The district endured significant destruction with the Great Kanto earthquake of 1923, yet again it continued to function until the Japanese government outlawed prostitution in 1958.[71]

Today, Yoshiwara resembles many other areas in modern Tokyo, but it nevertheless retains remnants of its history, with commercial establishments involved in the sex trade. The street grid pattern and old temples and shrines are still present.

---

[70] Kobayashi, Akira. "The Courtesans of Yoshiwara."
[71] "Yoshiwara." Wikipedia.

xiii. New Year's Day at the Ōgiya Brothel, Yoshiwara by Katsushika Hokusai circa 1804, panel 1. Public domain.

xiv. New Year's Day at the Ōgiya Brothel, Yoshiwara by Katsushika Hokusai circa 1804, panel 2. Public domain.

xv. New Year's Day at the Ōgiya Brothel, Yoshiwara by Katsushika Hokusai circa 1804, panel 3. Public domain.

xvi. New Year's Day at the Ōgiya Brothel, Yoshiwara by Katsushika Hokusai circa 1804, panel 4. Public domain.

xvii. New Year's Day at the Ōgiya Brothel, Yoshiwara by Katsushika Hokusai circa 1804, panel 5. Public domain.

The Yoshiwara Arson Incident

From 1676 to 1866, *Shin-Yoshiwara* (New Yoshiwara) experienced a total of twenty-two fires. The prevailing belief is that most of the fires were deliberate acts of arson initiated by the enslaved women working in the brothels. The fire that engulfed the brothel Umemotoya on August 5, 1849, is undoubtedly the most renowned.

In the latter half of the Edo period, Yoshiwara encountered an economic decline due to the proliferation of brothels in the city. These establishments, which did not have authorization from the shogunate, provided their services to patrons at considerably lower prices. When the shogunate began to crack down on these unofficial brothels in 1795, an alarming number of low-ranking prostitutes who had previously worked in them fled to Yoshiwara. As competition increased, the brothels where the district's prostitutes worked were forced to borrow money to continue operations, creating more difficult working conditions for the women. Naturally, the prostitutes were held accountable.

On a particular day known as "monbi," prostitutes in Yoshiwara demanded twice as much for their services. Holidays, including New Year's Day and Tanabata (also known as the Star Festival), were typical occasions for monbi. Nevertheless, in the absence of patrons, the girls were obligated to remit what they would have earned to the proprietors of the brothel.

Sakichi was the proprietor of the Umemotoya, and he had a reputation for being ruthless. He drove his girls mercilessly and when business suffered, so did they.[72] In September 1847, Tamashiba, a young sex worker, made an attempt to flee the Umemotoya. She was promptly apprehended and coerced into providing a false report. She was compelled to say that the *tayu* had given her money and had urged her to flee. Despite Tamashiba's initial defiance, Sakichi coerced her to comply by striking her on the head with a large iron, which inflicted severe pain and drove her to confess.

Toyohira, the tayu in question, entered the sex work industry at the age of thirteen. Ten years of diligent effort allowed her to rise to the top of the hierarchy. Her contract was to end in 1850, but Sakichi devised a scheme to prolong it. The following day, taking advantage of Tamashiba's false testimony, he filed charges against Toyohira in an effort to make an example out of her. In the presence of every other sex worker employed at Umemotoya, he subjected her to a violent assault.

He bound her hands, suspended her by her neck, and subjected her to forty-five blows with a bow stick. He abandoned her there, without any food or water. Toyohira was in excruciating pain, and the rope that had been fastened around her hands and neck had resulted in burn marks on her skin. Despite this, she maintained consciousness and resolve. Sakichi ultimately untied her after she assured him that she would prolong their contractual agreement by an additional two years.

Following this, Toyohira approached Tamashiba and requested a confession, promising to maintain the confidentiality of the information. Tamashiba disclosed that she had been coerced by Sakichi into providing a false testimony. Toyohira was a young woman renowned for her

---

[72] 吉原で最も有名な遊女「高尾太夫」と「16人の遊女たちの集団放火事件」/ "Yoshiwara's Most Famous Prostitute 'Tayu Takao' and the 'Mass Arson Incident of 16 Prostitutes.'" 草の実堂, 16 July 2022, kusanomido.com/study/history/japan/edo/59808.

altruistic nature. For example, there was an episode when she encountered a customer who was detained at a restaurant because he was unable to pay for the food he had ordered. Toyohira paid the man's bill in order to prevent him from being punished. She did not punish Tamashiba despite her betrayal. However, she harbored resentment towards Sakichi due to his brutal treatment and decided to seek revenge.[73]

She chose to set fire to the brothel to draw attention to the cruel treatment Sakichi imposed on the women who worked there. Tamashiba was one of the sixteen prostitutes who participated in her scheme. The following evening, while Sakichi slept, four prostitutes climbed to the second floor of the building and set fire to the ceiling. They decided to start the fire on the second floor because they thought it would be easier for people to see and put it out quickly.

Amidst the chaos of the fire, the sixteen women rushed to the town's authorities to confess and surrender. They were taken prisoner despite the fact that no one was killed in the fire. Arson was a grave offense that frequently resulted in a sentence of burning at the stake during the Edo period.

Judge Kagemoto Toyama imposed his sentences four months later. He rendered a relatively lenient judgment. In lieu of being burned at the stake, the four women who were directly responsible for the fire were exiled to a secluded island. Twelve others received prison sentences.

---

[73] Makino, Hiromi. "裁かれたのは誰なのか 吉原の遊女16人、集団放火その後/ "Who Was Judged after the Mass Arson of 16 Yoshiwara Prostitutes?" 毎日新聞, 毎日新聞/ Mainichi Shimbun , 6 Oct. 2021, mainichi.jp/articles/20211005/k00/00m/040/161000c.

Interestingly, the brothel owner did not escape the magistrate's judgement and was also banished to the island. It is believed that Toyama was well aware of the life in Yoshiwara and thus handed down lenient sentences.[74]

xviii. No. 9 Nectarine Brothel, Yoshiwara, circa 1910. Public domain.

---

[74] "吉原で最も有名な遊女「高尾太夫」と「16人の遊女たちの集団放火事件」/ Yoshiwara'sMost Famous Prostitute, Tayu Takao' and the 'Mass Arson Incident of 16 Prostitutes.'" 草の実堂, 16 July 2022, kusanomido.com/study/history/japan/edo/59808/.

xix. Sano Jirozaemon Murdering a Courtesan (1886) by Tsukioka Yoshitoshi, left panel. Public domain.

x. Sano Jirozaemon Murdering a Courtesan (1886) by Tsukioka Yoshitoshi, right panel. Public domain.

The Yoshiwara Killing Spree

Being a courtesan was a demanding and painful experience. After being abandoned by her family and forced into the sex trade, a courtesan faced the additional risk of physical violence from her procurer or patron. In 1696, the Yoshiwara courtesan Yatsuhashi was ruthlessly killed by her customer, Sano Jirozaemon.

There is a lack of information regarding Sano Jirozaemon. Numerous sources depict him as either a prosperous farmer or a wealthy charcoal wholesaler. The various accounts of the Yoshiwara killings, or *Yoshiwara Hyakunin Giri*, attribute the role of the perpetrator to the feudal ruler of Shimotsuke Province, presently incorporated within Tochigi Prefecture. What is certain is that he had strong feelings for Yatsuhashi and desired to pay her a visit. Nevertheless, Yatsuhashi declined to meet him as she was attending to another client. Jirozaemon became furious. He killed Yatsuhashi's client and slashed Yatsuhashi as well. He then turned his sword on a dozen or so courtesans trying to escape. Consumed by rage, he mercilessly took the lives of 100 individuals on that fateful day.

Jirozaemon then attempted to flee by scaling the brothel's roof, but he fell after being splashed with water. He was captured and promptly sentenced to death.[75]

---

[75] "佐野次郎左衛門 (Sano Jirozaemon)." Wikipedia, Wikimedia Foundation, 3 Sept. 2022, ja.wikipedia.org/wiki/%E4%BD%90%E9%87%8E%E6%AC%A1%E9%83%8E%E5%B7%A6%E8%A1%9B%E9%96%80.

The tragic incident inspired Kawatake Shinshichi III to pen a kabuki play titled *"Kagotsurube Sato no Eizame"* or "Kagotsurube the Haunted Sword."[76] The eight-act play, which premiered in May 1888, opens with the scene where Jirozaemon and his servant, Jiroku, watch the famous courtesan Yatsuhashi parade by with her attendants in tow. Though he is a simple countryman disfigured by smallpox scars, Jirozaemon falls in love with her at first sight.

He regularly visits her in Yoshiwara, and the two often meet at the Tachibanaya teahouse. Jirozaemon aspires to buy Yatsuhashi, thus relieving her of all financial obligations and setting her up as his mistress. However, the courtesan is currently in a romantic relationship with someone else.

Later, a celebration takes place at the Tachibanaya teahouse to commemorate Jirozaemon's successful freeing of Yatsuhashi. She welcomes Jirozaemon with an icy disposition and abruptly terminates the relationship, failing to provide an explanation for her behavior. Upon discovering her romantic involvement with another man, Jirozaemon proclaims his plan to abandon her and retreat to his countryside residence. Jirozaemon returns after a four-month absence, followed by the arrival of Yatsuhashi. The couple are alone in an upper room of the teahouse drinking sake together. Jirozaemon pours sake for Yatsuhashi and tells her to drink up as this will be her last time. Brandishing his sword, he slays both Yatsuhashi and the young girl who approaches carrying a lantern. Jirozaemon tries to escape, but is captured later.[77]

---

[76] "Tsujigiri." Wikipedia, Wikimedia Foundation, 19 June 2023, en.wikipedia.org/wiki/Tsujigiri.
[77] Richie, Donald. "KAGOTSURUBE." Kabuki21, www.kabuki21.com/kagotsurube.php. Accessed 16 Sept. 2023.

Jokan-ji: The Throwaway Temple

xx. The main gate of Jokan-ji

Jokan-ji, located a short distance from the Minowa Station on the Hibiya line in Tokyo, is an ordinary temple in the opinion of some. However, this temple has a comparatively dark past. It contains a memorial and a crypt honoring the twenty-five thousand prostitutes who were interred in its old cemetery. In the past, the brothel employees discarded the bodies of these women at the temple gates. As a result of the widespread adoption of this custom, the temple came to be referred to as *Nage Komi Dera* or the Throwaway Temple, which carried the connotation of a dumping grounds for unwanted and forgotten women.

Ansei Edo Jishin, or the Edo Earthquake of 1855, is considered to be the genesis of this practice.[78] The quake was the third major earthquake to strike Japan, taking place just one year after the Tokai Earthquake and the Nankai Earthquake of 1854.

The incident took place at 10:00 p.m. local time on November 11th, and the ensuing fires and tremors devastated the Kanto region. The number of fatalities is estimated to range from 7,000 to 10,000, while the destruction of 14,000 structures was documented. In addition, the earthquake generated a small tsunami.[79]

The women employed in Edo's pleasure quarter, Yoshiwara, were trapped and a significant number perished there, with some passing away during sexual intercourse. Yoshiwara was a walled area with two restricted exits that regulated the movement of people, which hindered evacuation during emergencies.

After the earthquake, there was a significant shortage of coffins. Many individuals, particularly those with the means, chose to create improvised coffins from sake barrels. On the other hand, the bodies of the ordinary prostitutes were stacked until they could be discreetly disposed. To avoid any adverse effects on the business, the women's bodies were secretly taken out the rear exit rather than being carried through the front gate in front of arriving customers. To reach the temple, the brothel workers

---

[78] Iles, Stuart. "The Throw Away Temple – Dumping Ground of the Yoshiwara Prostitutes." rekishinihon.com/2015/02/06/the-throw-away-temple-dumping-ground-of-the-yoshiwara-prostitutes/.
[79] "1855 Edo Earthquake." Wikipedia, 14 May 2023, en.wikipedia.org/wiki/1855_Edo_earthquake#:
~:text=The%201855%20Edo%20earthquake%20(%E5%AE%89%E6%94%BF, local%20time%20on%2011%20November.

bypassed the streets and took unmarked service routes through the rice paddies surrounding Yoshiwara.

Regrettably, the practice continued during the Meiji period (1868–1922) until Japan yielded to growing international pressure and made specific alterations in the Yoshiwara district. By 1905, the practice of dumping bodies at the temple was discontinued and a monument was erected for the women buried there. However, the temple's reputation as a dumping ground and the nickname Throwaway Temple remained.[80]

Throughout the Edo period, the Tokyo area was home to a number of throwaway temples: Saiho-ji in Toshima Ward, Taiso-ji and Jokaku-ji in Shinjuku Ward, Kaizo-ji and Hozen-ji in Shinagawa Ward, Sosan-ji in Kawasaki City, Monju-in in Itabashi Ward, and Unryu-ji in Hachioji City. Among these, Jokan-ji was the most prominent.[81]

At Jokan-ji, there stands a commemorative tower called *Shin-Yoshiwara Soreito*, which pays tribute to the women who were employed at Shin-Yoshiwara and perished during the 1855 Edo Earthquake. At first, a burial mound served as a memorial for the estimated 500 or more women who perished in Shin-Yoshiwara after the catastrophic earthquake. In 1929, Jokan-ji initiated the rebuilding of this mound, transforming it into the *Shin-Yoshiwara Soreito*. Engraved on its wall is a *senryu*, a Japanese form of poetry, by Hanamata Kasui. It reads:

> *"Born in hell, buried in Jokan-ji."* [82]

---

[80] Iles, Stuart. "The Throw Away Temple – Dumping Ground of the Yoshiwara Prostitutes."
[81] "投げ込み寺 (Nagekomidera)." Wikipedia, 16 Aug. 2020, ja.wikipedia.org/wiki/%E6%8A%95%E3%81%92%E8%BE%BC%E3%81%BF%E5%AF%BA.
[82] "Complete Guide: Jokanji Temple (Arakawa, Tokyo)." The Tokyo Shitamachi Guide, 15 May 2023, everywhere.tokyo/en/jokanji-temple/.

The poem presents evidence of the harsh existence faced by courtesans, not only in the Yoshiwara pleasure district but in all pleasure quarters established by the shogunate throughout Japan. These women were treated without any regard or dignity, even in their final moments.

Near the temple's inner gate is the grave of the renowned oiran, Komurasaki. She was a high-ranking courtesan who worked at the most prestigious brothel, Kadoebi-Ro, in Shin-Yoshiwara during the late 19th century.[83]

xxi. The crypt honoring the twenty-five thousand prostitutes in Jokan-ji.

---

[83] "Complete Guide: Jokanji Temple (Arakawa, Tokyo).".

Shimabara: Kyoto's Red-Light District

xxii. Willow Tree at the Gate of the Shimabara Pleasure Quarter, from the series "Famous Places in Kyoto" by Utagawa Hiroshige, circa 1834. Public domain.

Prior to its transformation into a *hanamachi* (geisha district), Shimabara was the designated red-light district in Kyoto. Founded in 1640, Shimabara ceased to function as a red-light district in the 1950s following the prohibition of prostitution in Japan. By the 1970s, there was no official record of any geisha in Shimabara. Tayu, who never really left the quarter, were given the opportunity to register as a separate category of geisha in 1956 with the passing of the *Baishun boshi ho* (The Prostitution Prevention Law). Currently, they are still performing within the ward. Shimabara now operates as a tourist district and is home to only two *ochaya* (tea houses).

The name Shimabara likely originated from its prominent eastern gate, which shared similarities with the gate of Shimabara Castle in Hizen. Alternatively, it is possible that due to its chaotic foundation, the name was intended as a reference to the just concluded *Shimabara Rebellion* (1637–38).

During the Tokugawa period, this area was also known as *go-men no ocho* (the licensed quarter, or the quarter) differentiating its high-class workers from the unlicensed women who conducted business in the surrounding cities. Sex workers, unlike those in the other pleasure quarters, were permitted to enter and leave the district after obtaining a pass. Ordinary individuals, regardless of their gender, were also granted the freedom to come and go as they pleased.

Due to the Meiji restoration and the subsequent transfer of the imperial court to Tokyo, many traditional enterprises in Kyoto that catered to the aristocrats faced economic challenges. Unlike the five hanamachi that successfully adjusted and continue to exist today, Shimabara gradually declined over the following century and eventually stopped operating as a geisha district in the 1970s. However, some traditional activities still continue to this day. The primary factor contributing to this decline can be attributed to the isolation of Shimabara. Established on the outskirts of the city, the district remains rather far and inconvenient to reach compared to the more centrally located districts.

Like other geisha districts in Kyoto, Shimabara also featured a dance venue where an annual performance called *Aoyagi odori* (Green Willow

Dance) took place. The dance was performed between 1873 and 1881; its end coincided with the waning of enthusiasm for dancing in the area. The dance hall moved to another venue in 1927 and was repurposed as an office space after World War II. Ultimately, it was demolished in 1996.

In 1976, Shimabara disassociated itself from the Kyoto Hanamachi Association after being devoid of a resident geisha population. The structure that housed the dance hall until 1927 has been converted into a convalescent home. Two teahouses, the *Sumiya* (1641) and the *Wachigaiya* (1688), which have been preserved as cultural assets, remain.[84]

Operating as both an *okiya*[85] and a teahouse, only Wachigaiya holds an official teahouse license. Originally founded in 1688, the okiya was known as Yokaro. In 1872, the ochaya business was incorporated. Since its 1857 reconstruction, the current structure has remained essentially unchanged. Its umbrella room features sliding doors embellished with the umbrellas that are traditionally used during tayu parades. Another room is referred to as the "room of autumn leaves," and features tracings of autumn leaves on its walls.

The institution, which was previously staffed with geisha, now serves as a training facility for tayu. Furthermore, the building functions as a venue for hosting banquets. There is a sign affixed to the front door that reads "Ichigensan Okotowari," indicating that no guests are allowed. Only individuals who have been "introduced" are permitted to enter as new

---

[84] "Shimabara, Kyoto." Wikipedia, 9 Sept. 2022, en.wikipedia.org/wiki/Shimabara,_Kyoto.
[85] An okiya (置屋) is the lodging house/drinking establishment to which a maiko or geisha is affiliated.

clients. Kyoto City officially designated the structure as a registered cultural property in 1984.[86]

Notable tayu linked to Shimabara include Sakuragi Dayu, Yachiyo Dayu, Yoshino Dayu, and Yugiri Dayu. In the former Shimabara area, a yearly October memorial is held to pay tribute to Yoshino Dayu and Yachiyo Dayu.

Currently, there are five tayu who work for the Wachigaiya: Hanaogi Dayu, Kisaragi Dayu, Usugumo Dayu, Wakagumo Dayu, and Sakuragi Dayu. They engage in the tayu procession, while also performing dances in the tatami room of the Wachigaiya tea house, shrines, and temples in Kyoto. Like the maiko and geisha of Gion, the present tayu also uses white face makeup, with red lipstick being only applied to her bottom lip. Their teeth are usually blackened and they do not use wigs. Their obi sash is recognizably secured at the front in a pentagonal configuration, representing the kanji character for heart.[87]

---

[86] Yu, A. C. "Wachigaiya (the Name of a Tea House) - Japanese Wiki Corpus." Wachigaiya (the Name of a Tea House) - Japanese Wiki Corpus, www.japanesewiki.com/building/Wachigaiya%20(the%20name%20of%20a%20tea%20house).html. Accessed 16 Dec. 2023.
[87] "島原 (京都) (Shimabara (Kyoto))." Wikipedia, Wikimedia Foundation, 11 June 2023, ja.wikipedia.org/wiki/%E5%B3%B6%E5%8E%9F_(%E4%BA%AC%E9%83%BD).

Shinmachi: Osaka's Red-Light District

xxiii. Nakanoshima in Osaka. Creative Commons Attribution-Share Alike 4.0 International license

Shinmachi was Osaka's foremost pleasure district, founded between 1615 and 1623. It continued to operate until its destruction in World War II. The site was situated about two kilometers (1.2 miles) to the southwest of Nakanoshima, a narrow sandbank in Kita-ku, Osaka City, that divides the Kyu-Yodo River into the Tosabori and Dojima rivers. Currently, it mostly functions as a tourist attraction.[88] It is worth noting that during the Edo

---

[88] "Shinmachi." Wikipedia, 12 Oct. 2022, en.wikipedia.org/wiki/Shinmachi.

period, there was no separate town called "Shinmachi," and the term "Shinmachi" only referred to the Shinmachi red-light district.

In 1615, right after the *Siege of Osaka*, Matajiro Kimura, a *ronin* (a masterless samurai) from Fushimi Town, petitioned the shogunate to open a brothel. After receiving authorization, he consolidated the prostitutes scattered throughout Osaka City and opened a brothel to the south of the Dotonbori River. Unlike Yoshiwara, which was geographically separated from Edo, and Shimabara, which was surrounded by agricultural fields, Shinmachi was located in the heart of the city. Yoshiwara and Shimabara each had one gate, whereas Shinmachi had seven gates.

In the Genroku era (1688-1704), Shinmachi was home to around 800 prostitutes, including tayu. The pleasure quarter thrived until the start of the Meiji era. Shinmachi began to decline starting with the creation of the Matsushima red-light district in 1869, followed by the *Emancipation Order for Geisha and Prostitutes* in 1872, and the Great Fire of September 5, 1890.

Following the Meiji period, the Shinmachi red-light district gradually transformed into a commercial zone, with shops proliferating in the district's core and an increase in the number of wholesalers specializing in mechanical and metal tools. In 1922, the Yoshidaya brothel was the only one still in existence. The Ageya Takashimaya establishment closed, and the Shinmachi Enbujo kabuki theater was built in its place. Finally, in 1945, the *Great Osaka Air Raid* devastated the city, reducing the old Shinmachi area to ashes.

After the war, the effort of reconstructing Osaka began. Naniwa-suji Road was constructed over the former Shinmachi area, erasing the district's distinct streets and characteristics. However, Naniwa Horie 1500, a non-profit organization based in Osaka, has painstakingly recreated a model of the Shinmachi red-light district using authentic historical artifacts. The model was later exhibited in the Osaka City Library.

Shinmachi was an important part of Osaka's cultural environment during the Edo period, used as a backdrop for various literary works by renowned authors including Ihara Saikaku and Chikamatsu Monzaemon. The pleasure quarter also serves as the setting for the renowned *rakugo* (form of Japanese verbal entertainment, traditionally performed in yose theatres) tale known as "Winter Play."[89]

---

[89] "新町遊廓 (Shinmachi Red Light District)." Wikipedia, Wikimedia Foundation, 6 Sept. 2023, ja.wikipedia.org/wiki/%E6%96%B0%E7%94%BA%E9%81%8A%E5%BB%93.

Furuichi: Ise's Red-Light District

xxiv. The Bizen-ya teahouse in Furuichi, Ise, circa the 1890s. Photographer unknown, public domain.

Ise, formerly known as Ujiyamada, is a Japanese city located in the central part of Mie Prefecture. It houses *Ise Jingu* (the Ise Grand Shrine), the ancestral shrine of the Japanese monarchs and the most sacred Shinto shrine in Japan.[90]

Established in 4 BCE, Ise Jingu is comprised of two distinct shrines, namely the *Naiku*, which signifies the inner shrine, and the *Geku*, which signifies the outer shrine. *Furuichi Sangu Kaido*, a pilgrimage route that traverses the historic entertainment district of Furuichi, connects the two

---

[90] "Ise, Mie." Wikipedia, Wikimedia Foundation, 23 June 2023, en.wikipedia.org/wiki/Ise,_Mie.

principal shrines. Since the road was frequently used by pilgrims on their way to Ise Jingu, the town grew to include brothels, restaurants, and inns that catered to the travelers.[91]

During the Edo period, the Tokugawa government imposed strict travel regulations on all citizens, regardless of social class. *The Sakoku* (literally "chained country") period in Japan's history arose when Japan's isolationist stance severely limited relations and trade with other countries. The policy prohibited almost all foreign nationals from entering Japan and prevented ordinary Japanese citizens from leaving the country. The Tokugawa shogunate also exercised unprecedented control over all aspects of national travel in the pre-industrial era. All ordinary Japanese citizens were required to obtain a permit to travel. But despite the difficulties in acquiring permits and the high cost of travel, tourism still thrived during the Edo period.

Trailing behind business travel, religious pilgrimage was the second most prevalent purpose for travel throughout the Edo era. Indeed, Edo period literature is rife with satires about pilgrims whose sole religious practice was purchasing a handful of amulets at the temple to prove they had been there. Most pilgrims were likely sincere in their devotion, but their visit to the shrine was frequently part of a relaxing holiday. Among those who could afford it, vacations lasting several months, leisurely wandering around Japan from one famous sight to another, were quite common.[92]

---

[91] Cartwright, Mark. "Ise Grand Shrine." World History Encyclopedia, https://www.worldhistory.org#organization, 15 Sept. 2023, www.worldhistory.org/Ise_Grand_Shrine/.

[92] Ohkubo, Kristine. "The Substitute Dog (Okage-Inu) - Japanup! Magazine." JapanUp! Magazine - Informational Site for Japan Fans, 28 Sept. 2022, japanupmagazine.com/archives/6989?fbclid=IwAR0hN6J0IudXCtNHRyipus_mFIhTcogj3WR9Tbg_80igy8IRH8Xve3_V5Sc.

During the Edo period, Furuichi was home to the third most renowned red-light district, following Yoshiwara in Edo and Shimabara in Kyoto. In the early Edo period, the red-light district consisted of only six teahouses. It expanded in size and prominence over the course of the Edo period. By 1704, Furuichi's red-light district included 60 teahouses and 162 courtesans. By 1789, the district had grown to include 70 teahouses and 1,000 courtesans. The Sugimoto-ya, Abura-ya, and Bizen-ya were the most popular teahouses at the time.

Today, Furuichi's teahouses, inns, playhouses, and other colorful amusement spots, which blossomed during the Edo period, are mostly gone. Instead, travelers to Furuichi will find several stone markers identifying historical sites, such as the ones commemorating the Aburaya brothel and the shamisen players, Osugi and Otama, who entertained the pilgrims during the mid-Edo period. Surprisingly, the Asakichi Ryokan (inn), which is more than two centuries old, still stands, providing visitors with a glimpse into the neighborhood as it once was.[93]

---

[93] "Furuichi." Furuichi - SamuraiWiki, 2010, samurai-archives.com/wiki/Furuichi.

xxv. The actors Fujikawa Tomokichi II and Onoe Matsusuke II playing the roles of the courtesan Okon and Fukuoka Mitsugi by Utagawa Kunisada I, panel 1. Public domain.

xxvi. The actors Fujikawa Tomokichi II and Onoe Matsusuke II playing the roles of the courtesan Okon and Fukuoka Mitsugi by Utagawa Kunisada I, panel 2. Public domain.

The Abura-ya Riot

Throughout history, violence has been a pervasive phenomenon in Japan's pleasure quarters, including the red-light district of Furuichi. On May 4, 1796, a dispute ensued that resulted in nine stabbings; this incident later came to be known as the *Abura-ya Riot*. Information about the Abura-ya Riot was rapidly disseminated throughout Japan, largely due to the influx of pilgrims who traversed the Furuichi Sangu Kaido to reach the Ise Shrine.

The Abura-ya was a well-known brothel in Furuichi that accommodated twenty-four prostitutes, each with their own private chamber. The event concerned a 27-year-old resident physician called Magofuku Itsuki.

Magofuku Itsuki, originally named Yokichi, was born as the second child of Yojiemon, a farmer hailing from Toba Matsuo (currently known as the Matsuo district in the municipality of Toba, Mie Prefecture). After being adopted into the Toba clan by Yojiemon's brother-in-law, he was named Itsuki. Itsuki studied medicine in Kyoto. After graduating, he received a residence in Uratacho, where he established his practice.

Itsuki visited the Abura-ya teahouse at around 1:00 a.m. on May 4, 1796, where he was served sake. Due to his frequent patronage, he was guided to the tatami room, where he requested the company of Okon, a sixteen-year-old courtesan. It was at that time that Iwajiro (33 years old), Magosaburo (35 years old), and Itaro (31 years old), three merchants from Awa, stopped by the Abura-ya on their way home after seeing a play. Okon received an invitation to join them, accompanied by another courtesan. Itsuki expressed strong indignation and lodged a formal protest regarding Okon's removal to the other clients' quarters. Oman, the 26-year-old maidservant, pacified him and instructed him to return to his residence, guiding him towards Abura-ya's main entrance.

As Itsuki was leaving, Oman promptly returned the *wakizashi* (a short sword) that Itsuki had relinquished upon entering the premises. She sustained injury to three fingers of her left hand when Itsuki suddenly struck her with the sword. Ukichi, a 30-year-old male servant, had his right thumb amputated while attempting to stop Itsuki.

Itsuki thereafter directed his attention towards Oyoshi, a 40-year-old servant, and slashed him to death. Saki, the 58-year-old mother of Abur-ya's proprietor, Seiemon, was among those he killed upon invading the Abura-ya's interior.

The merchants who were drinking with Okon, and the others in the parlor on the second floor, overheard the commotion. Okishi was the first person to make his way to the first floor; upon doing so, Itsuki fatally stabbed him, then turned his sword on Okon. Despite suffering injuries to her right shoulder and forehead, Okon managed to escape through the rear entrance. While attempting to subdue Itsuki, Itaro sustained cuts to his right arm and buttocks; Magosaburo suffered lacerations to his left eye, lip, right shoulder, and back. After suffering a laceration to the left arm, Iwajiro made an effort to escape upstairs but was pursued by Itsuki, which ultimately resulted in his death.

With an injured hand, the servant Ukichi emerged from the brothel and ordered the neighbors to execute Itsuki; however, he evaded capture and disappeared. On the evening of May 6, Itsuki was discovered in the residence of Fujinami, a low-ranking priest in Uratacho. After squeezing through the parlor's paneling, he allegedly committed suicide by slashing his stomach and stabbing himself in the throat with a blade. His whereabouts prior to that day are unknown; nevertheless, there were noticeable differences in his attire and belongings between the time he was discovered at the Fujinami residence on the 6th and his visit to the Abura-ya on the 4th. These differences indicate that he might have had some form of interaction with someone. It is likely that he was concealed. In contrast, Okon lived to the age of 49. She died on February 9, 1829.

"Ise Ondo Koi no Netaba," a kabuki play based on the incident, made its debut on July 25, 1796.The title roughly translates as "The Ise Dances and Love's Dull Blade." The story features a cursed Shimosaka sword which, once it is drawn, must taste blood.

Itsuki and Okon are thought to be buried together in Furuichi's Dairin-ji Temple. Their final resting place is known as the "lover's grave."

The Abura-ya was renovated and converted into an inn during the Meiji period. However, in order to clear space for the Kintetsu Toba Railway Line, it was subsequently demolished.[94]

---

[94] "油屋騒動 (Aburaya Riot)." Wikipedia, Wikimedia Foundation, 24 Apr. 2023, ja.wikipedia.org/wiki/%E6%B2%B9%E5%B1%8B%E9%A8%92%E5%8B%95.

Dairin-ji Temple

xxvii. The lover's grave at Dairin-ji Temple, Furuichi

Situated in the Furuichi district of Ise City, Dairin-ji is a Jodo-shu Nishiyama Zen temple that was established sometime between 1614 and 1625. It is the region's earliest surviving temple. Originally constructed on a mountain road, the temple was relocated to the town near the red-light district in 1691, an area with which it remained inextricably linked.

On June 27, 1852, a young monk's recklessness caused a fire that quickly spread and destroyed 280 buildings.[95] At that time, the district was home

---

[95] "Dairinji." Dairinji - SamuraiWiki, 2010, samurai-archives.com/wiki/Dairinji.

to 40 tea houses and 780 courtesans. Four years later, the temple underwent reconstruction in a more refined and modern design.

In 1869, during the Meiji period, the temple was abandoned and its Buddhist sculptures, altars, and other sacred objects were disseminated to more than 160 other temples as part of the anti-Buddhism movement supported by the government. Since the reestablishment of Dairin-ji in 1894, certain buildings have undergone renovations while others have been relocated.

The temple is arguably best known for its association with the kabuki drama "Ise Ondo Koi no Netaba" and the incident that inspired its creation. A local physician named Magofuku Itsuki, who in 1796 went on a murderous rampage in the nearby Abura-ya teahouse, is believed to be interred in a lover's grave at Dairin-ji alongside his beloved, the courtesan Okon. Due to its proximity to the former teahouse, the temple has become a popular tourist attraction among kabuki enthusiasts. Prominent kabuki actors who portray Itsuki (Mitsugi) and Okon frequently visit this sacred site to pay their respects.

An offerings box, and a modest prayer hall known as *Aizendo* (Love-Stained Hall), once stood in front of the couple's monument; however, both were destroyed during a typhoon and never rebuilt. The primary artifact once venerated in the demolished hall, an Aizen-Myo statue, was recovered and relocated to a newly constructed hall.

The Dairin-ji Aizen-Myo was the primary patron deity guarding the Furuichi red-light district, and it remains a patron deity or protector of the local restaurants and nightlife establishments to this day. Paper lanterns, which were generously supplied by a group of Kamigata (Kansai) kabuki actors, line the pathway connecting the tomb to the main street.[96]

---

[96] "Dairinji." Dairinji - SamuraiWiki.

Maruyama: Nagasaki's Red-Light District

xxviii. Maruyama brothel, circa the 1890s. Public domain.

Although Yoshiwara is the most widely-known pleasure quarter to have existed in Japan, followed by Shimabara and Shinmachi, there was a prominent, yet less often discussed courtesan district in Nagasaki known as Maruyama. The Maruyama pleasure quarter was officially established in 1641 with the goal of concentrating all of the city's prostitutes into two distinct wards: Maruyama and Yoriai. The courtesans of Maruyama mostly served the Chinese and Dutch populations who lived in the port city.

Once established, the women of the pleasure quarter were granted access to the Dutch community of Dejima, which had not seen any women for several years. Only the courtesans of Maruyama, together with shogunate officials, were granted access to the Dutch neighborhood on Dejima. These women also offered their services to Chinese merchants, Japanese nationals, and travelers from various regions of the island country that visited Nagasaki.

Originally, the courtesans were mandated to depart from Dejima in the morning and were strictly prohibited from spending the night in the Chinese neighborhood. However, these laws were rarely enforced and became increasingly lenient during the Edo era. Consequently, courtesans were eventually allowed to reside in foreign settlements indefinitely, as long as their patrons continued to provide financial support and the courtesans themselves desired to remain there.

The girls assigned to each group were deliberately kept apart to prevent any collaboration or collusion in smuggling or conspiracies between the Dutch and Chinese communities. As a result, certain Maruyama courtesans earned the moniker of *karayuki* ("Miss Gone to China"), catering only to Chinese and Japanese clientele, while others, known as *orandayuki* ("Miss Gone to Holland"), served only Dutch and Japanese clients. A select few of the most prestigious Maruyama courtesans only catered to Japanese clientele and were referred to as *nihonyuki*, meaning "Miss Gone to Japan."

Though they could not smuggle goods, money, or information between the Dutch and the Chinese, the women of the pleasure quarter were able to carry things between the foreign districts and the Japanese townspeople of Nagasaki, thus circumventing the shogunate's clearinghouse, which claimed monopolies on a variety of trade goods, and charged high tariffs.

The courtesans were also given personal gifts by their clients, some of which were rare and valuable, such as white sugar from Indonesian plantations or different types of textiles. Although the authorities mandated that these gifts be declared to prevent smuggling, they also stated that these gifts belonged to the courtesans and could not be seized by the brothel owners.

The courtesans were known to favor the Chinese over the Dutch due to the significant cultural differences, including sexual preferences, personal hygiene practices, and overall culture. Consequently, the orandayuki charged higher fees to their Dutch patrons compared to the karayuki who served Chinese clients.

Enforcement of restrictions on the island were quite lax at times, and on occasion, courtesans even escorted Dutchmen off Dejima (into Nagasaki proper), or accompanied them out of the country. Several Maruyama courtesans also bore offspring with men from the Dejima community. Certain children from Maruyama were assimilated into Japanese society and considered "Japanese," either because they were raised within Maruyama or by the courtesan's parents. These children remained in Japan for their entire lives, facing the same restrictions on leaving as any other Japanese citizen. On the other hand, some children of Maruyama courtesans were classified as foreigners and lived either on Dejima or outside of Japan for the rest of their lives. They were prohibited from entering or freely traveling within Japan, just like any other foreigner.

In contrast to the girls who were sent to other prominent pleasure quarters, it appears that the girls from Maruyama managed to maintain strong familial connections. They procured and transported various items to provide for their families. Also, in specific situations, they were often successful in garnering support from the authorities to address unjust treatment or to terminate their contracts in order to reintegrate into mainstream society, establish marital relationships, and start families.

Some girls, who were Maruyama prostitutes serving the Chinese and Dutch communities, had the option to remain at home and only go out to Dejima or the Chinese enclosure when the brothel they were affiliated with needed more girls to meet the demand for a particular night. Allowing the girls to work part-time, or while still living with their parents, concerned the authorities because it created ambiguity between the "ordinary" townspeople, who were barred from entering foreign areas, and the prostitutes, who were not subject to such restrictions. As a result, occasionally, women engaging in part-time prostitution were captured and fined, usually by being forced to undertake unpaid work on a full-time basis in Maruyama.[97]

By 1680, there were 54 brothels in Maruyama, with 776 prostitutes, including 127 tayu. In 1692, the number of prostitutes reached its highest point of 1,443. The economy of Maruyama changed in direct proportion to its trade with China and Holland. By the end of the Edo period economic activity remained sluggish, with only 28 brothels housing a total of 487 female workers.

---

[97] "Maruyama." Maruyama - SamuraiWiki, 2016, samurai-archives.com/wiki/Maruyama.

Between 1830 and 1844, a tayu's fee was 70 momme of silver, which is equivalent to 15,000 yen ($105) in today's currency. In addition, the costs of a luxurious supper and many other goods were included, resulting in a threefold increase in the final amount. [98]

Engelbert Kaempfer (1651-1716) and Carl Peter Thunberg (1743-1828), both physicians working for the Dutch East India Company, gave extensive reports of Maruyama during their assignments on Dejima in 1691-92 and 1775-76 respectively. Within Kaempfer's comprehensive publication, we encounter a particular excerpt that seemingly contradicts our understanding of societal attitudes towards a prostitute.

The area of Nagasaki where the brothels are located is known as Kesiematz, (keisei-machi), which translates to the Bawdy Houses Quarters. It lies to the South, on a rising hill, called Mariam (Maruyama).

According to the Japanese, it comprises two streets that may appear to a European as more than two. These streets are home to the most attractive private buildings in the entire town, all occupied by those involved in the sex trade.

There are only two public brothels, known as Mariams, in Saikokf (Saikoku, i.e. Kyushu), including one in the province Tsikusen. Although not as well-known, these establishments offer a place where the less fortunate people of this island, which is known for producing the most beautiful women in all of Japan (with the exception of the women of Miaco/Miyako, i.e. Kyoto, who are said to be even more beautiful), can

---

[98] "Forgotten Foibles: Love and the Dutch at Dejima (1641–1854)." Forgotten Foibles: Love and the Dutch at Dejima (1641–1854) | East Asian History, 2021, www.eastasianhistory.org/39/vos-foibles/index.html.

sell their daughters if they are attractive and have pleasing physical features.

The trade here is significantly more lucrative than anywhere else, primarily due to the large influx of foreigners who are only permitted to visit Nagasaki. Additionally, the local residents themselves are reputed to be the most indulgent and promiscuous individuals in the entire Empire.

The girls are acquired from their parents at a very young age. The price is directly correlated with the attractiveness of the commodity and the duration of the agreed-upon period, typically ranging from ten to twenty years, give or take.

Each procurer maintains a maximum number of individuals, ranging from seven to thirty, in a single residence. The children are comfortably accommodated in attractive rooms, and significant effort is made to instruct them in dancing, singing, playing musical instruments, writing letters, and all other necessary skills for their intended lifestyle.

The older individuals, possessing greater ability and expertise, provide guidance to the younger ones, who in turn serve them as their apprentices. Individuals who demonstrate significant advancements in their education, possess physical attractiveness, and exhibit pleasant conduct are frequently selected and summoned, resulting in substantial benefits for their instructors. Additionally, these individuals are provided with clothing and accommodation, all of which are funded by their admirers, who must pay a higher price for their affections as a result.

The sum of money given to their landlord ranges from one Maas to two Itzebi per night, and they are strictly prohibited from requesting any amount beyond that, with the risk of facing severe fines. One of the most pitiful individuals, who is almost exhausted from excessive use, must guard the home throughout the night in a little room next to the door, where any traveler may have dealings with her, for a fee of only one Maas. Others are assigned to perform guard duty as a kind of punishment for their misconduct.

Upon completing their term of service, if they are married, these individuals are perceived as respectable women by the general population. The blame for their previous immoral lifestyle is not attributed to them, but rather to their parents and relatives who sold them into such a disgraceful means of earning a living during their early childhood, before they had the ability to choose a more honorable path. In addition, their often-refined upbringing improves their ability to choose suitable spouses.[99]

Thunberg gave the following account of Maruyama:

Many Japanese cities have multiple residences dedicated to the worship of the Cyprian Goddess, located on specific streets, mostly for the entertainment of travelers and other individuals. The town of Nagasaki is no different in this regard, as it provides opportunity for the Dutch and Chinese to spend their money in ways that are not considered respectable.

If an individual seeks a companion during their retirement, they express their desire to a specific individual who visits the island daily for the purpose of fulfilling this request. Prior to the evening, this gentleman acquires the company of a young woman, who is accompanied by a

---

[99] "Forgotten Foibles: Love and the Dutch at Dejima (1641–1854)."

subordinate female servant commonly referred to as a Kabro (kamuro). The Kabro is responsible for daily trips to the town to gather all the necessary food and beverages for her mistress. Additionally, she prepares meals, brews tea, maintains cleanliness and organization, and fulfills various errands.

One of these female companions must be retained for a minimum of three days, but can be kept for as long as desired, whether it be a year or even several years consecutively. After a certain period of time, one is allowed to make a change. However, in this situation, the woman must present herself daily at the town gate and notify the authorities whether she intends to remain on the island or not. Each day, a sum of eight mas is given to the lady's husband, while she herself occasionally receives gifts like silk robes, girdles, and head jewels, in addition to her regular support.

Undoubtedly, Christians, who are guided by their religious and moral principles, should refrain from engaging in immoral relationships with the unfortunate young ladies of this nation. However, the Japanese, who are Heathens, do not consider lasciviousness to be a moral failing, especially at establishments that are sanctioned by the legal system and the government. Therefore, houses of this nature are not seen as disreputable establishments or inappropriate meeting locations. These establishments are commonly visited by individuals of higher social standing who desire to entertain their acquaintances with sakki (sake).

Impoverished parents, who have an abundance of daughters they cannot support, engage in the practice of selling their daughters to individuals when they reach the age of four years or older. During their early childhood, they work as domestic servants in the household, specifically serving the older women, with each lady having her own personal attendant.

When a young woman reaches the age of twelve, fifteen, or sixteen, she is then celebrated and often at the cost of the person she served during the previous years, to become one of those privileged ladies who are relieved from serving others or engaging in any form of work.

Instances where these women conceive children with Europeans are extremely rare. However, if such an occurrence were to happen, it was believed that the child, particularly if male, would be subject to infanticide. Some individuals said that these youngsters were closely monitored until the age of fifteen, after which they were taken to Batavia on ships. However, I find it difficult to imagine that the Japanese would engage in such inhumane practices, and there is no evidence to support the occurrence of the latter.

While residing in this country, I encountered a young girl approximately six years old who had a striking resemblance to her European father. She lived on our small island for the entire year alongside him.[100]

A child born to a German national working in Dejima and a Nagasaki prostitute became the first female practitioner of contemporary medicine in Japan. Kusumoto Ine was her name.[101]

---

[100] "Forgotten Foibles: Love and the Dutch at Dejima (1641–1854)."
[101] "Kusumoto Ine." Wikipedia, 13 Sept. 2021, en.wikipedia.org/wiki/Kusumoto_Ine

The Pre-1750 Hierarchy of Courtesans

Tayu

The highest echelon of courtesans. The word originated in the Shimabara district of Kyoto and then became prevalent in Osaka, Edo, and Nagasaki. To engage the services of a tayu, one had to first complete a series of long processes and rituals. These include obtaining a recommendation letter from one of the teahouses and submitting an application to the *ageya*, the establishment to which the tayu was affiliated.

Koshi

The second tier of courtesans. Acquiring the services of a koshi involved a series of steps akin to those for seeking a tayu, only shorter and less challenging. The koshi and her attendants would have a meeting with the client on a single occasion, in contrast to the tayu who would meet with the customer three times, prior to making a determination regarding accepting him as a client.

Tsubone

These were courtesans of lower status, priced at around one-tenth the cost of a koshi. The customers could not be refused, and there was no need for a formal application process. The girls were displayed in the latticed front-room of a brothel, waiting for customers to select them. Each tsubone had a dedicated chamber allocated for her use as well as for the benefit of her clients.[102]

---

[102] "Courtesans." Courtesans - SamuraiWiki, samurai-archives.com/w/index.php?title=Courtesans&mobileaction=toggle_view_desktop. Accessed 2 Feb. 2024.

The Post-1750 Hierarchy of Courtesans

Chusan
Their customer base consisted of wealthy businessmen and government dignitaries. The *agedai,* or fee, was equivalent to a minimum of 130,000 yen ($885) in current-day currency.

Zashikimochi
Merchants were among the clientele of these courtesans, who operated their own parlors. The *agedai* usually exceeded 50,000 yen ($340).

Heyamochi
Included among their clientele were shogunate and feudal retainers. The accommodations for courtesans were basic single rooms. The *agedai* exceeded 25,000 yen ($170).

Furisode Shinzo

They were not provided with private rooms, but rather shared large quarters. Patrons were individually attended to in a designated space known as a *mawashibeya*.

Tomesode Shinzo

Their circumstances were similar to the furisode shinzo, but with no opportunity for advancement to the upper ranks.

Banto Shinzo

Prostitutes who had reached their mid-twenties, and thus exceeded the maximum age, continued to reside in Yoshiwara. In lieu of receiving patrons, they served as managers for the oiran.

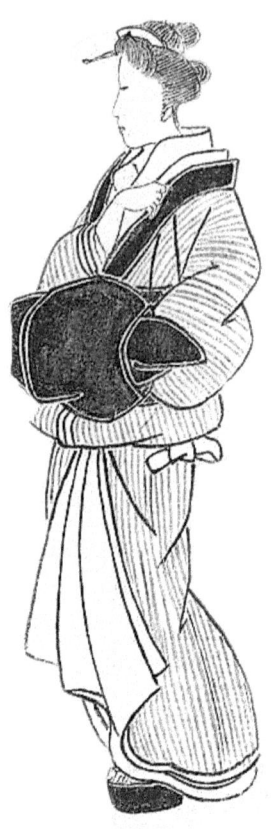

Kamuro

These adolescent females would subsequently engage in prostitution. In their mid-teens, they initiated the transition to shinzo.[103]

---
[103] Kobayashi, Akira. "The Courtesans of Yoshiwara."

Life of a Courtesan

A significant number of women working in the pleasure quarters during the Edo period were forced into their occupation. Their parents, who were engaged in agriculture or fisheries and experienced financial hardships, sold them to brothels. The girls were typically indentured to the brothel proprietors at the age of seven to nine years. In exchange for a fixed sum of money, the parents entered into a ten-year agreement with the proprietors of the brothel, during which time the girls were obligated to work in order to repay the loans.[104]

Upon their arrival at the brothel, the young girls were assigned daily responsibilities, which included cleaning, delivering messages, and tending to their elder sister courtesans. Additionally, they acquired practical knowledge and skills during those formative years, such as how to use manipulative language and write love letters.[105]

The girls who had demonstrated exceptional skill or ability by the age of eleven or twelve would be selected to undergo specialized training to become courtesans. The course of study would consist of a diverse range of lessons, such as playing the flute or the *shamisen* (a three-stringed instrument comparable in tone to the banjo), singing, dancing, calligraphy, painting, haiku poetry composition, tea ceremony performance, and backgammon gameplay. To stimulate her patrons' interest, the elite courtesan was required to have a comprehensive

---

[104] Hix, Lisa. "Sex and Suffering: The Tragic Life of the Japanese Courtesan."
[105] Hix, Lisa. "Sex and Suffering: The Tragic Life of the Japanese Courtesan."

knowledge of literature. Men would find her more attractive as she gained more skills. In a brothel, the degree of opulence and personal space accorded to an elite courtesan were contingent on her level of expertise.[106]

Once the girls were admitted into courtesan training, their virginity was auctioned off to the highest bidder. The majority of the young adolescent courtesans' clientele consisted of clients who were waiting to meet with a top courtesan. Eventually, they would become competitors vying for clients and the top position. The courtesans participated in fierce rivalry, often displaying acts of cruelty toward their competitors. At times, their customers mistreated them and subjected them to abhorrent abuse.[107]

Additionally, some of the girls were subjected to mistreatment by the proprietors of the establishments where they were employed. As the mistreatment of prostitutes reached an unprecedented level by the late 18th century, new regulations were mandated by the authorities. As per one of the regulations:

> *"Among the proprietors of the houses of prostitution, there are those who administer corporal punishment to their prostitutes. A certain amount of control and discipline is necessary, but it is far beyond normal behavior to torture a prostitute for not being able to secure clients on fete days."*[108]

Even after the implementation of new regulations, the use of physical force against prostitutes remained legal. A casual tap on the wrist was administered as punishment to brothel proprietors who were accused of

---

[106] Hix, Lisa. "Sex and Suffering: The Tragic Life of the Japanese Courtesan."
[107] Hix, Lisa. "Sex and Suffering: The Tragic Life of the Japanese Courtesan."
[108] Seigle, Cecilia Segawa. "Corporal Punishment and Other Abuses." *Yoshiwara: The Glittering World of the Japanese Courtesan*, University of Hawaii, Honolulu, HI, 1993, p. 211.

mistreating the women. Legal repercussions for such treatment were limited to situations in which the mistreatment resulted in the death of a prostitute.[109]

The *tayu*, who held the most esteemed status in the realm of courtesans, symbolized the elite class of the pleasure districts. Some tayu held positions as concubines and courtesans for the imperial princes, and unlike lower-ranking courtesans, they were given permission to enter the palace. And in their leisure time, the princes went on horseback or by palanquin to amuse themselves at the famous pleasure quarters where the tayu lived.[110]

In order to enjoy the company of a tayu, a man needed to first submit an application for a meeting at an *ageya*, which functioned as a house of assignment before the establishment of teahouses in the geisha districts. A wealthy man would ask for a certain tayu by name; some tayu were in such high demand that it could take several months to secure an appointment on their calendar. The owner of the ageya would draft a letter addressed to the bordello where the courtesan resided, and subsequently hand it over to a messenger to deliver. The customer would partake in the revelry of dancing girls and jesters while he waited his turn. Additionally, he would purchase food and beverages for them, all of which would be applied to his tab.

Hours later, after having made their way down the boulevard at a snail's pace as onlookers ogled, the tayu, wearing countless layers of exquisite kimonos and opulent hair ornaments, entered with her retinue. The

---

[109] Seigle, Cecilia Segawa. The Glittering World of the Japanese Courtesan.
[110] Hix, Lisa. "Sex and Suffering: The Tragic Life of the Japanese Courtesan."

procession to meet the client is known as an *oiran dochu*. Its main purpose was to advertise the houses where the high-ranking courtesans worked.

During their first meeting, tayu and customer passed their time by engaging in activities such as dancing, sharing poems, enjoying music, and participating in the tea ceremony. Sex did not automatically follow. Ultimately, the courtesan's value would be diminished if she were too easily available. The proprietor who owned the tayu would seek to maximize her exclusivity in order to increase the value of his or her investment. In order to engage in sexual relations with the courtesan, the client would be obligated to undertake an extensive and costly courtship. It was unrealistic to expect to engage in sexual activity with her prior to the third visit.[111] Furthermore, if the tayu was unsatisfied with the man's performance, she retained the authority to refuse to engage in sexual relations with him. If she agreed to his proposition of spending the night, she demanded a payment of 90 silver pieces, which is equivalent to approximately $675 in current currency. Despite the considerable expense involved, affluent men persisted in their pursuit of tayu, and they were the only demographic that a tayu would consider.[112]

Putting aside the allure associated with a tayu, it is critical to understand that a considerable number of the prostitutes suffered from tuberculosis, syphilis, or both. At times, the establishments experienced outbreaks of typhoid fever. Overall, reaching the age of thirty was an exceptionally rare occurrence for a common courtesan.[113]

---

[111] Hix, Lisa. "Sex and Suffering: The Tragic Life of the Japanese Courtesan."
[112] Hix, Lisa. "Sex and Suffering: The Tragic Life of the Japanese Courtesan."
[113] Iles, Stuart. "The Throw Away Temple – Dumping Ground of the Yoshiwara Prostitutes." Japanese History and Culture: Educational Studies of Japanese History,.

Those who contracted venereal disease were stigmatized with the label "confined to a chicken coop."[114] There was a premodern Japanese satirical genre called *sharebon*, which can be roughly translated as "book of manners." Its production spanned from the 1720s until the end of the 18th century. The narratives featured in the book were predominantly set in Yoshiwara and revolved around the misfortunes of two male prototypes who represented contrasting qualities: the *tanketsu*, or those who merely pretended to be refined, and the *tsu*, who were truly sophisticated.[115]

The *sharebon* publications referred to the alarming prevalence of venereal diseases. A story illustrates this point when, while waiting for his courtesan, a client is literally scared to death upon encountering a grotesque white apparition with disheveled hair. Later on, it is disclosed that the apparition is that of a prostitute from the adjacent room who had wandered out at night in search of food after being confined to the chicken coop without care or attention.[116]

Unsurprisingly, the death of a prostitute was not met with much lamentation or public display of sorrow. A woman of that social status was neither interred in a casket nor accorded a formal burial ceremony. Oftentimes, workers in brothels quickly found a place outside the pleasure quarters to get rid of the dead body. They wrapped the corpse in a cheap rush mat before disposing of the body.

Although the women working in the brothels had legally binding contracts for a specific length of time, they were deliberately subjugated

---

[114] Seigle, Cecilia Segawa. The Glittering World of the Japanese Courtesan.
[115] "Sharebon." Wikipedia, 4 Mar. 2023, en.wikipedia.org/wiki/Sharebon.
[116] Seigle, Cecilia Segawa. The Glittering World of the Japanese Courtesan.

to further work by debts that they were unable to fully repay. As the young women progressed in their professions as courtesans, they found themselves accumulating more debt instead of making payments toward their existing loans. The responsibility for covering the costs of their opulent kimonos, as well as the gratuities and fees for their attendants, fell upon them. They were compelled to work for long stretches, including during periods of illness or menstruation, in order to meet their daily work quota. The quotas doubled on holidays and if the girls failed to make them, they were fined. If they missed a day's work for any reason at all, they had to pay the bordello the sum they would have earned if they had worked. They were only allowed to leave the brothel for the death of a parent and once a year to view the cherry blossoms.[117]

Most carried on working until they were twenty-seven, the usual retirement age. If a girl was lucky, her contract might be bought out by a wealthy patron, allowing her to transition from brothel sex worker to the position of mistress or spouse of the man to whom she was sold.[118]

---

[117] " Downer, Lesley. "Women of the Pleasure Quarters-The Secret History of the Geisha."
[118] Hix, Lisa. "Sex and Suffering: The Tragic Life of the Japanese Courtesan."

xxix. Lower-level prostitutes displayed in wooden latticed cages known as harimise in Yoshiwara, circa 1889. Photographer unknown, public domain.

xxx. Men entering the Nectarine No. 9 brothel in Yoshiwara with prostitutes standing on the balconies, circa 1889. Photographer unknown, public domain.

xxxi. Satogiku Dayu with kamuro (child attendants), circa 1910. Public domain.

The Kamuro

The great courtesans of Japan's pleasure quarters were accompanied by young girls known as *kamuro* (child attendants). Before reaching the age of nine, they were enlisted to serve as attendants to their "elder sister" courtesan. Their duties included accompanying her in public, running errands on her behalf, and joining her in meetings with clients. In the pleasure district, one would frequently observe young girls dressed in vibrant clothing hurrying through the streets. They delivered gifts, relayed orders to merchants, visited vendors, engaged in friendly banter with locals, and bought snacks for the courtesans to quickly eat in between attending to clients.

As one might expect, the kamuro were protected and cared for, while nonetheless exposed to the harsh reality of life in the pleasure quarter. They were cognizant of the means by which their older sisters supported themselves. They exhibited their usefulness in specific occasions. For example, a client might inquire with his preferred courtesan's kamuro about her feelings towards him. As an innocent child, the kamuro could be trusted to tell the truth, and the client would be made to feel as though the courtesan was in love with him. For a kamuro, learning to play these games constituted an important part of her education, alongside her calligraphy and music training.

Unlike *maiko* (an apprentice geisha), who also had an older sister, the kamuro were solely the responsibility of their older sisters. The maiko-older sister dynamic is predominately one of a ceremonial nature. While the geisha acquaints the younger sister with society, imparts etiquette guidance, and aids in her social integration, the maiko's *okiya* (the lodging house to which a maiko or geisha is affiliated with during her career) finances her debut, housing, meals, kimono, and hair ornaments. However, it was the courtesan's responsibility to ensure that her kamuro was adequately clothed, fed, and protected. A kamuro would have perished if the courtesan failed to work. Additionally, if the kamuro were to make her first appearance as a courtesan, the exorbitant expenses would be covered by her older sister.

It is important to mention that although the courtesan had financial responsibility for her kamuro, she did not possess ownership of the kamuro's contract. The courtesan's brothel procured the young girl. However, the girls were not necessarily contracted by the brothel owners for the duration of their working lives. The brothel owners frequently engaged the girls for a limited time as kamuro, a contractual arrangement that prevented them from having to advance substantial sums of money for girls who did not fulfill their initial commitment.

It was expected that once the girl was prepared to enter the profession of prostitution, her contract would be renewed for the standard ten-year period for a prostitute. However, her parents or procurer might arrive at the contract negotiation with a better offer from a different brothel. The brothel-keepers were powerless to prevent them from removing her and selling her to another brothel, and thus transferring all the resources of time and money that had been invested in her education. For many girls, this situation may have appeared beneficial. Brothels were categorized based on the ranks of the courtesans they hired. A highly skilled girl would have had more chances to achieve her goals if she worked at a higher-ranked establishment. However, in the event that a lower-ranking house extended a greater financial offer to the girl's parents, she might lose the chance to become a courtesan at all. Most kamuro were not reclaimed and resold by their parents, which can be seen as either fortunate or unfortunate. Upon finishing their tenure as kamuro, they commenced their work at the very same brothel where they had spent their formative years.

Kamuro served as powerful symbols of the elite. They were solely employed as attendants to the most distinguished courtesans. At first, courtesans were only allowed to have one kamuro. However, in the early 1700s, Miyakoji, a daring courtesan, started parading with two kamuro. When questioned by the individuals responsible for enforcing the restrictions of the pleasure district over this extraordinary demonstration of extravagance, she courteously explained that she owned only one kamuro, while the other one belonged to one of her fellow courtesans. Consequently, it became trendy to be seen with two kamuro, but it was implied that only one of them actually belonged to the courtesan in question.

A new rule was eventually codified by the authorities: the highest-ranking courtesans were permitted two kamuro, while those of lower rank were limited to one. Ordinary prostitutes of any rank were prohibited from possessing any kamuro.

To symbolize the courtesan's social status, kamuro were carefully paired together. They were ideally of the same height, had identically styled hair (or one girl was assigned a girl's hairstyle while the other was assigned a boy's hairstyle), were adorned in kimonos and ornaments that matched, and were given names that matched.[119]

Unlike the very elaborate names of the courtesans, kamuro had simple names. The katakana script, deemed childlike and less elegant, was primarily employed in lieu of the more refined kanji. Examples of matched names include: Hanano and Haruno (Flowery Field and Spring Field), Onami and Menami (Big Waves and Little Waves), Kanomo and Konomo, and Takeno and Sasano.

Although courtesans may have had several attendants available to them, often only their kamuro were mentioned by name in advertisements. The *shinzo*, or apprentice courtesans, were almost never mentioned by name. It is reasonable for the courtesans to want to downplay the importance of their shinzo, since they were in direct competition with them. Conversely, they would want to emphasize their kamuro, as they served as the eyes and ears of their older sisters in the district.

A courtesan dedicated most of her time to serving clients, and during the breaks between appointments, she refrained from aimlessly wandering around the area. The shinzo had a similarly busy work schedule. In contrast, the majority of a kamuro's time was spent out in the streets. Every individual connected to their brothel was familiar with the kamuro. Potential clients might interact with them openly, subtly exchanging witty remarks and inquiring about their older sisters. The young girls were not hesitant to grab onto a man's sleeve and implore him to revisit their elder sister or to prolong his stay in the brothel after he had finished. Unlike the

---

[119] Issendai. "Kamuro." Kamuro | Japanese Courtesans | Issendai.Com, 2013, www.issendai.com/japanese-courtesans/kamuro.html.

older brothel staff, they did not insist on receiving significant gratuities from customers.

A man may regularly engage with a courtesan's kamuro, both within and outside the brothel. Therefore, including the names of her kamuro alongside hers could serve as a means to alert him of which young child to approach.[120]

---

[120] "Kamuro." Kamuro | Japanese Courtesans | Issendai.Com, 2013, www.issendai.com/japanese-courtesans/kamuro.html.

xxxii. Oiran dochu, Yoshiwara, circa 1920. Public domain.

The Oiran

The highest-ranking courtesans in both the Shinmachi and Shimabara districts of Osaka and Kyoto were referred to as *tayu*. In contrast, they were referred to as *oiran* in Edo. One possible explanation for the word oiran is that it is a diminutive form of *oira no tokoro no nēsan*, which translates to "the older sisters of our place." At first, Yoshiwara used the name tayu, but around the mid-eighteenth century, the term oiran started being used instead.[121]

An oiran's appeal in the pleasure quarter was contingent upon her physical attractiveness, charisma, intellect, and artistic aptitude. Upon attaining the position, oiran would often be bestowed with generational names known as *myoseki*, which were exclusively owned by the proprietor of the brothel. Historically, these names were typically associated with those who had a similar reputation and status. Being promoted to the position of an oiran symbolized the transfer of that person's prestige. Myoseki, composed of kanji characters, were typically adopted for the purpose of safeguarding one's identity or promoting the brothel's image. Poetry, literary history, and nature provided the metaphorical connotations for these names, which frequently possessed a delicate, more elaborate quality than the average feminine name. Also, it was not customary for an oiron to transfer her myoseki to her trainees.

Compared to geisha and average women, oiran displayed a markedly distinctive aesthetic by reflecting the preferences and expectations of their

---

[121] Kobayashi, Akira. "The Courtesans of Yoshiwara."

affluent clientele. During the Edo period, oiran, who were at the peak of their profession, embellished their hairstyles with eight or more large *kanzashi*, which were ornamental hair accessories made from materials such as tortoiseshell, silver, gold, and jewels. These hairstyles, each with its own name and significance, were worn to represent different seasons and occasions.

An oiran's attire consisted of multiple kimono layers, with the *uchikake* being the outermost kimono. The uchikake was made of silk brocade and included intricate embroidery and a padded hem. Although uchikake were eventually adopted by some brides and noblewomen towards the end of the Meiji period, oiran wore significantly more opulent and vibrant versions.

The uchikake were adorned with luxurious gold and silver thread embroidery, showcasing intricate and symbolic motifs such as dragons, butterflies, arabesque rondels, pine trees, plum blossoms, and bamboo. This was to be worn without a belt over the *juban* (a component of the kimono undergarments), which only featured a patterned design on the lower skirt. An *obi* sash was employed to secure the outfit in the front. During the Edo period, the obi became wider and stiffer, which caused more discomfort and added weight. Oiran earned a reputation for donning a particular style of obi called the *manaita obi* (literally "cutting board obi"). This obi featured an expansive, level surface upon which meaningful designs were embroidered.

When parading or otherwise walking, oiran wore 20 cm (7.9 in) tall *koma geta* (wooden clogs) with three "teeth." Though lightweight for their size, these would prevent an oiran from taking anything other than small, slow steps when walking. Oiran would thus walk in *koma geta* with a sliding, figure eight (*suri-ashi*) step, with two manservants (known as *wakaimono*) assisting her. In general, oiran refrained from donning *tabi socks* (traditional Japanese socks worn with thronged footwear), as her bare feet were regarded as an erotic element of her appearance. An oiran's formal parade attire could frequently weigh between 20 kg (44 lb.) and 30 kg (66 lb.). It also required assistance to put on.

With a reputation for providing exclusive and high-priced entertainment, oiran predominantly catered to the affluent. In fact, the oiran was financially unattainable for the majority of men. One ryo and one bu, which is equivalent to 130,000 yen ($885) today, was required to spend the night with the highest-ranking *chusan*. Additionally, the proprietors of the establishment demanded substantial gratuities. A client could potentially pay gratuities upwards of one million yen ($6,808) in today's currency prior to engaging in sexual relations with the oiran.[122]

Their perceived ability to captivate upper-class men and challenge their intelligence earned oiran the nickname "castle toppler." A considerable number of oiran achieved recognition within the realm of the pleasure quarters and beyond it; they were often depicted in ukiyo-e woodblock prints and kabuki theater productions.

In addition to conversing with clients in a formalized upper-class language, oiran were expected to possess a comprehensive understanding of classical dance, music, and traditional singing, as well as the ability to play the *kokyu* (a traditional Japanese string instrument resembling a

---

[122] Kobayashi, Akira. "The Courtesans of Yoshiwara."

banjo, but played with a bow) and the *koto* (a Japanese plucked half-tube zither instrument).[123]

It was customary to pay three visits prior to being granted permission for the initial evening of pleasure. During this period, monetary gifts and presents of obi belts or kanzashi hair ornaments were required.[124] The oiran would sit far away from the customer during the first visit and would not eat, drink, or converse with him. During this period, the oiran would determine whether or not the client was worthy of her services. To demonstrate his wealth, the prospective client summoned a large number of women and consumed ample amounts of food and alcohol.

The oiran would position herself closer to the customer during the second meeting. As before, the process would remain unchanged. She would not eat, drink, or converse with him. Once again, the client would gather other girls and revel excessively to demonstrate his affluence and power. The patron would become a *najimi*, or a familiar patron, during the third encounter. The oiran would perform her duty during the third meeting.

The oiran, in contrast to a typical prostitute, chose her clients. She assumed the *kamiza* position during banquets, whereas her client assumed the *shimoza* position. The kamiza is occupied by those of higher social standing in Japan. Nevertheless, this differentiation was only observed within the walls of Yoshiwara.[125]

Despite being regarded as trailblazing and fashionable women in their prime, during the late 18th and early 19th centuries, the status of the oiran

---

[123] "Oiran." Wikipedia, 22 Apr. 2023, en.wikipedia.org/wiki/Oiran.
[124] Kobayashi, Akira. "The Courtesans of Yoshiwara."
[125] Sakowako, Y. "20 Facts You Did Not Know about Oiran." Tsunagu Japan, 2015, www.tsunagujapan.com/20-facts-you-did-not-know-about-oiran/.

was supplanted by geisha. The merchant classes were captivated by the simplicity of the geisha's attire, their adeptness at performing contemporary melodies known as "kouta" on the shamisen, and the more stylish portrayals of modern womanhood. The companionship they provided reflected the tastes of the ultra-wealthy.

On the other hand, as a result of their isolation in the pleasure quarter and rigid courtesan contracts (which often extended for ten to fifteen years before their retirement), oiran progressively became more antiquated, and ritualized. Eventually, they became more and more estranged from mainstream society and confined by their stringent etiquette, conduct, and language requirements. This, coupled with their relative financial inaccessibility to the majority, created a vacuum of entertainment for the rising merchant classes. Their relatively low social standing and high wealth prevented them from engaging oiran, which prompted them to opt for the considerably more accessible and affordable geisha.

As time passed, oiran also experienced a decline in their celebrity status within society at large. They were perceived not as refined courtesans exemplifying formal, affluent standards of attire and conduct, but rather as women confined to the pleasure quarters and obligated to repay the debts owed to their brothel.

In addition, the preservation of the oiran's aesthetic was unable to keep pace with changes in fashion, whereas the geisha profession grew in prominence and complexity. Several dress edicts issued by governing bodies in an effort to control the ostentatious and affluent tastes of the merchant class altered the prevailing aesthetics and spawned more refined and subdued styles, which the oiran neither mirrored nor resembled.

In a similar fashion, the entertainment provided by oiran had largely persisted unaltered over the course of previous generations of courtesans. While oiran played the shamisen, they refrained from performing contemporary and well-known pieces composed for the instrument. Instead, they opted to perform long ballads like *nagauta*, which featured lyrical content that was refined yet restrained. This was in contrast to the *kouta* (little songs) that were revered and performed by geisha, featuring lyrical content that frequently conveyed sincerity and openness.

The popularity and numbers of oiran continued to decline steadily throughout the 19th century before prostitution was outlawed in Japan in 1957. Nevertheless, the tayu who prevailed in the Shimabara district of Kyoto were granted permission to keep participating in the artistic and cultural customs associated with their vocation. Moreover, they were regarded as a special variety of geisha. A limited number of tayu, who abstain from prostitution in the course of their duties, continue to exhibit their art in Kyoto. This is in addition to several oiran reenactors from other regions of Japan who present the *oiran dochu*, which are reenactments of courtesan parades.[126]

Oiran dochu/ Soto-Hachimonji

When an oiran was summoned for service, she met her client after a slow and ritualistic procession with her kamuro and shinzo. The tayu and, subsequently, the oiran led the *oiran dochu* procession, which showcased the courtesan in her ceremonial garb, including her most recent uchikake and highest geta sandals. It included her entire retinue, entrusted with the responsibility of transporting her pipe, tobacco box, and additional

---

[126] "Oiran." Wikipedia.

accoutrements. The shinzo participated in the parade not only to flaunt the prestige of their older sister courtesan, but also to attract potential customers of their own. The courtesan, however, also required male attendants: one to carry her enormous umbrella adorned with her *kamon* (crest), ensuring visibility from a distance, and another to provide a place for her to rest her hand as she executed the figure-of-eight step.

These were private parades commissioned by an extraordinarily affluent patron willing to finance the courtesan's retinue. Additional fringe groups, such as street merchants offering confections for sale to spectators and artists selling ukiyo-e prints depicting the courtesan in procession, derived benefits from the *dochu*.

By the end of the Edo period, these displays of wealth were no longer regarded as fashionable, despite the fact that wealthy and powerful men may have been willing to invest in such a spectacle, especially since oiran parades ultimately served to elevate the patrons' status. So, the oiran adapted by eliminating superfluous attendants. The only people that remained in the procession were her kamuro, her male *hikifune* (which served as her support), and an umbrella-bearer.[127]

---

[127] Geimaiko. "The Figure Eight Walk." GeiMaiko, 19 July 2020, geimaiko.tumblr.com/post/624055474380210176/the-figure-eight-walk#:~:text=Oiran%20%2D%20Soto%20Hachi%20ji&text=The%20Oiran's%20walking%20style%20is,damage%20to%20her%20expensive%20footwear.

xxxiii. Takao Dayu II by Utagawa Hiroshige, (1797-1858). Public domain.

Takao Dayu II

Takao Dayu (1640–1659), also known as Sendai Dayu, was one of the most celebrated courtesans during the Edo era. After her debut in 1655 as the leading courtesan of the Miuraya, the largest and most esteemed brothel in Yoshiwara, she quickly ascended to the position of tayu.[128] She was an elegant woman, famous for her expertise in poetry and calligraphy, who showed a sense of detachment towards her extremely wealthy customers. Date Tsunamune (1640–1711), a samurai from the early Edo period and the third *daimyo* (feudal lord and subject of the shogun) of the Sendai domain, was drawn to this particular trait. Having fallen in love with her, he resolved to claim her as his own.[129]

Date Tsunamune became a daimyo at the age of eighteen, following his father's death. He was the subject of swiftly spreading rumors that questioned his ability to lead due to his lack of expertise and his inclination towards alcohol and women. Date Munekatsu, his uncle, was at the forefront of the opposition. Legend has it that the clever uncle accompanied Tsunamune to Yoshiwara, where Tsunamune developed a strong and ardent love for Takao.[130]

Takao, however, was in love with a warrior belonging to the Tottori clan. Although he lacked the means to buy her freedom, they had made a solemn vow to marry once Takao had fully settled her debt with Miuraya.

---

[128] "Takao II." Wikipedia, 12 Mar. 2023, en.wikipedia.org/wiki/Takao_II.
[129] "The Tragic Lives of the 5 Most Famous Oiran - Can You Imagine the Cruel Truth? With En Subtitles." YouTube, 27 Aug. 2022, www.youtube.com/watch?v=_Y5vc8MmgNE.
[130] "Date Tsunamune." Wikipedia, 2 Feb. 2021, en.wikipedia.org/wiki/Date_Tsunamune.

As a result, she rejected Tsunamune's proposal to buy her out of her contract.

However, the greedy owner of the brothel made a deal with Tsunamune to forcibly take Takao away for a sum of 500 million yen (equivalent to around $5 million).[131] According to legend, Tsunamune offered to buy Takao's contract by paying her weight in gold. The dishonest brothel owner manipulated him into paying an excessively high sum by placing weights in her sleeves.[132]

According to one narrative, Takao was compelled to depart from Yoshiwara alongside Tsunamune, however she adamantly avoided any physical contact with him. Tsunamune made concerted efforts for a period of six months to sway Takao's opinion, but she unequivocally rejected his romantic advances. Frustrated, he imprisoned her and threatened to torture her. When this failed, he placed her in a boat and set sail on the Sumida River. There he suspended Takao upside down and hacked her to pieces.[133] Still another version says that Tsunamune had one of her fingers broken for every day she refused his bed, and after he had gone through both hands, he had her hanged.[134]

According to another account, Takao allegedly threw herself into the river as Tsunamune came to take her to his house. He pierced her in the heart after removing her by her hair from the river in a fit of rage. Tsunamune's uncle and the other conspirators took advantage of the opportunity to expose him to the authorities and force him to resign. This story gave rise

---

[131] "The Tragic Lives of the 5 Most Famous Oiran."
[132] Date Tsunamune." Wikipedia.
[133] "The Tragic Lives of the 5 Most Famous Oiran."
[134] McNeill, Maggie. "Takao." The Honest Courtesan, 24 Mar. 2015, maggiemcneill.com/2015/03/24/takao/.

to an array of *bunraku* (a form of traditional Japanese puppet theatre) and kabuki performances.

Throughout the years, a significant number of researchers have endeavored to determine the veracity of these legends. They deduced that Tsunamune did pay a visit to Yoshiwara and was mesmerized by Takao; however, it seems that she passed away on December 5, 1659, due to tuberculosis rather than by his hand.[135]

xxxiv. Ukiyo-e print depicting Date Tsunamune slaying Takao Dayu. Artist unknown, public domain.

---

[135] "Date Tsunamune." Wikipedia.

xxxv. Portrait of Date Tsunamune. Artist unknown, public domain.

xxxvi. The Courtesan Usugumo Holding a Cat by Tsukioka Yoshitoshi, circa 1876. Public domain

Usugumo Dayu

There were three courtesans in Yoshiwara who were all named Usugumo Dayu. The name's origin is credited to the novel *The Tale of Genji*, which was written by Murasaki Shikibu, a noblewoman, poet, and lady-in-waiting, during the Heian period (794-1185). "Usugumo" is the translation of the phrase "Wisps of Cloud" and serves as the title for the 19th chapter of the novel.

According to historical records, it may be inferred that the Usugumo in question was a second or third generation courtesan. This conclusion is based on the fact that the first generation Usugumo worked as a tayu in Yoshiwara from 1658 to 1661.[136]

While there is limited information available about her life, it is known that she hailed from Shinshu (present-day Nagano prefecture) and had a strong affection for a calico cat named Tama.[137] Tama and Usugumo were inseparable. When Usugumo paraded in the oiran dochu to meet her clients in the evening, the cat also traipsed alongside her.

Due to the superstitious disposition of the locals, tales quickly spread that Usugumo had been possessed by the cat, a *kaibyo* (a supernatural cat in Japanese folklore). During that period, the Japanese maintained the belief that deceased cats had the ability to metamorphose into *yokai*, or paranormal entity with the power to manipulate humans.

---

[136] Nyugen. "Usugumo Tayu: Tama, The Calico Cat from Which the Maneki Neko Is Derived." RSS, 24 Apr. 2019, monspedia.com/usugumo/.
[137] Nyugen. "Usugumo Tayu: Tama, The Calico Cat from Which the Maneki Neko Is Derived."

One day, Tama accompanied Usugumo to the bathroom, as cats often do. The proprietor of the brothel witnessed this and, using a sword, he severed the feline's head. Usugumo reportedly escaped a terrible fate when the severed head of Tama rolled into the soil pit and bit the head of a snake who was lurking there.

Devastated, Usugumo buried her cherished companion. She erected a statue made of *kyara*, the highest grade of Aloeswood used for making high quality incense, over its grave. *Kyara* was also the archaic Japanese term meaning "precious."

Tama is said to have been the inspiration for the renowned *maneki neko* (beckoning cat) of Japan, which is believed to bestow good fortune upon its owner.

Ultimately, Usugumo's contract with the Miuraya brothel was purchased for a sum of 35 million yen ($350,000). Her benefactor remains unidentified and her whereabouts after leaving Yoshiwara are unknown.

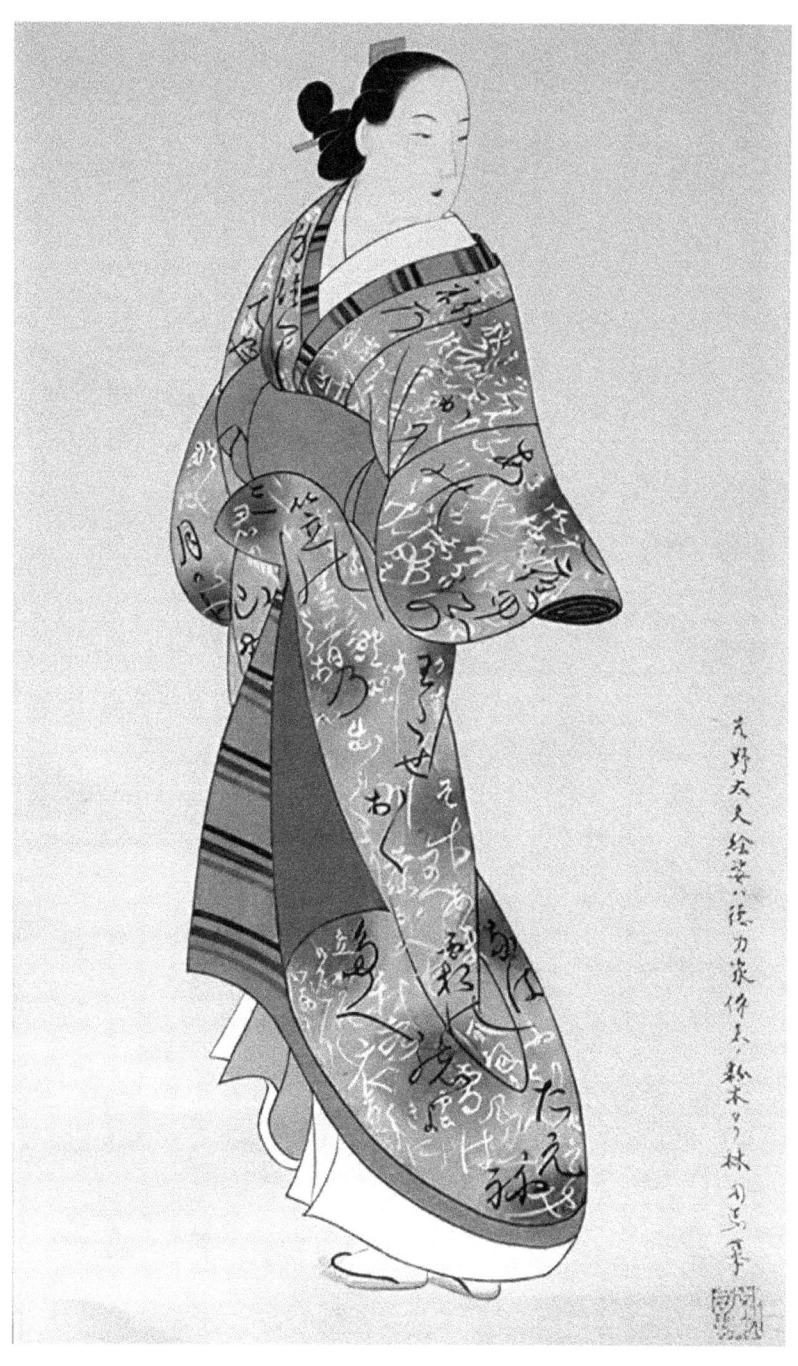

xxxvii. Yoshino Tayu (2nd generation), Joshoji Temple collection. Public domain.

Yoshino Dayu II

According to folklore, Yoshino Dayu II (1606-1643) was the child of a samurai from the western province of Yamashiro (modern-day Kyoto Prefecture). Her real name was Matsuda Tokuko, and she was taken in as a child by the Hayashiya brothel where she worked as a kamuro.

Yoshino, a remarkably perceptive person, quickly developed expertise in several musical instruments, including the *biwa* (a Japanese lute), the *koto* (a classic Japanese zither), and the *sho* (a wind instrument similar to panpipes). Aside from her expertise in the tea ceremony, incense ceremony, and flower arrangement, she was also admired for her exceptional literary skills and calligraphy. Yoshino was also proficient in playing *Sugoroku*, a Japanese version of backgammon, *Kaiawase*, a game from the Heian period that involves matching the two halves of clamshells, and *Go*. Her remarkable skill at playing Go earned her acclaim not just in Japan, but also in China, where she was highly sought after.

By the time she turned fourteen, her extraordinary beauty and talents had elevated her to the prestigious position of tayu. Konoe Nobuhiro (1599–1649), a Japanese court noble and the fourth son of the 107th Emperor of Japan, Emperor Go-Yozei, was among her regular clients.[138]

---

[138] Yu, A. C. "Yoshino Tayu (a Courtesan of the Highest Rank) - Japanese Wiki Corpus." Yoshino Tayu (a Courtesan of the Highest Rank) - Japanese Wiki Corpus, www.japanesewiki.com/literature/Yoshino%20Tayu%20(a%20courtesan%20of%20the%20highest%20rank).html. Accessed 18 May 2023.

According to legend, the apprentice of a skilled sword maker was driven out from Shimabara after he offered his entire savings of 80,000 yen ($800) in exchange for spending a night with Yoshino. She felt compassion toward him and secretly extended an invitation for him to spend the night with her.[139]

In 1631, after ending her career as a prostitute, Yoshino married Haiya Joeki (sometimes spelled Haiya Shoeki), a merchant who had been a regular customer. Sadly, Yoshino died in 1643 at the age of 37. Her remains were interred at Josho-ji Temple, a Buddhist temple affiliated with the Nichiren sect, located in the northwestern region of Kyoto. Yoshino, a devoted adherent of Nichiren Buddhism, reportedly provided financial support for the construction of Yoshino-mon, a grand vermilion gate that now stands at the entrance to the temple.[140]

---

[139] "The Tragic Lives of the 5 Most Famous Oiran - Can You Imagine the Cruel Truth?"
[140] Yu, A. C. "Yoshino Tayu (a Courtesan of the Highest Rank) - Japanese Wiki Corpus."

Katsuyama Dayu

Katsuyama, who began her career in 1646 as a low-ranking sex worker in a bathhouse named Tanzen, rose rapidly through the courtesan hierarchy and became one of the most influential fashion pioneers of the Edo period. Tanzen was shut down by the authorities in 1653 following a violent clash between residents and rival samurai. Katsuyama was recruited by a prominent Yoshiwara brothel, which quickly promoted her to the rank of tayu.[141]

While participating in the oiran dochu procession one day, a bold onlooker slashed her hair tie. Unfazed, Katsuyama sought refuge in a nearby teahouse, where she tied her hair into a knot with the help of her assistant. To secure it in place, she improvised using a chopstick. When she resumed her oiran dochu, spectators were in awe of her appearance and the wives of samurai and wealthy merchants quickly rushed to copy her look. Her profound influence on fashion led to individuals quickly capitalizing on her fame by adorning an assortment of items, including geta sandal straps and obi belts, with her name.

Katsuyama also embraced men's clothing, potentially setting a pattern for subsequent feminist movements. Her unwavering character led her to decline engaging in flirtatious behavior with her clientele. She also adamantly rejected all offers to purchase her contract with the brothel.[142]

---

[141] Downer, Lesley. "Women of the Pleasure Quarters-The Secret History of the Geisha."
[142] "The Tragic Lives of the 5 Most Famous Oiran - Can You Imagine the Cruel Truth?"

xxxviii. Komurasaki Dayu by Hosoda Eishi, circa 1794. Public domain.

Komurasaki Dayu

Komurasaki Dayu, a courtesan and respected waka[143] poet, took her name from Murasaki Shikibu, a famous Heian period poet and author renowned for *The Tale of Genji*. The work of fiction chronicles the life of Hikaru Genji, who was born to a low-ranking concubine named Kiritsubo Consort and was the son of an ancient Japanese emperor.

Komurasaki had feelings for a man named Hirai Gongen, but he was too poor to visit Yoshiwara. To get the money he needed to visit Komurasaki, he resorted to a series of robberies that ultimately resulted in a murder. Gongen was later apprehended and executed for his crimes.

Upon receiving news of her lover's death, Komurasaki slipped into a deep state of depression. Still, her greedy brothel owner was able to negotiate the purchase of her contract.

Tragically, Komurasaki committed suicide on the day she was supposed to leave Yoshiwara with the man who had bought her contract.[144]

---

[143] A short poem with specific structural requirements, written to express feelings.
[144] "The Tragic Lives of the 5 Most Famous Oiran - Can You Imagine the Cruel Truth?"

Ohashi Dayu

Ohashi Dayu, whose given name was Ritsu, worked in the Kyoto red-light district of Shimabara. In Edo, her father once held the rank of *hatamoto*, which refers to a distinguished samurai who worked directly for the shogun. Unfortunately, his fortunes quickly changed, and he became a *ronin* (a masterless samurai). After the family relocated to Kyoto, Ohashi was sold to a brothel in Shimabara.

Her exceptional education as the daughter of a samurai enabled her to quickly ascend the courtesan hierarchy. Ohashi had exceptional skills in calligraphy and poetry composition. Over time, Ohashi's contract with the brothel was bought out, allowing her to retire.

Following the death of her redeemer, Ohashi wed Kazumoto Kurihara. After becoming a disciple of the Reizei family, a Kyoto court noble lineage with a lengthy poetic heritage, she commenced her study of *waka* poetry. Later in life she converted to Buddhism, and under the tutelage of the monk Ekaku Hakuin, she became a Zen nun.[145]

---

[145] "大橋太夫." ("Tayu Ohashi"). Wikipedia, Wikimedia Foundation, 15 June 2021, ja.wikipedia.org/wiki/%E5%A4%A7%E6%A9%8B%E5%A4%AA%E5%A4%AB.

Sakuragi Dayu

Sakuragi Dayu was a poet and tayu who worked at the Wachigaiya tea house in the Shimabara pleasure quarter at the end of the Edo period.

Today, the Wachigaiya, which was founded in 1688, and the Sumiya are the only remaining tea houses in the area that was formerly a pleasure quarter. As the Wachigaiya continues to host tayu and geisha from other districts, it is not accessible to the general public. The Sumiya, on the other hand, has been transformed into a publicly accessible museum.[146]

Sakuragi later gained notoriety as the "famous flower of the Meiji Restoration" and was the mistress of prominent Meiji era reformers, including Ito Hirobumi, Japan's first prime minister, and Katsura Kogoro (later Kido Takayoshi). Kido, in his capacity as *san'yo* (Imperial Advisor), played a significant role in the establishment of the new Meiji government.

Following the assassination of Ito by Korean nationalist An Jung-geun at the Harbin railway station on October 26, 1909, Sakuragi renounced her worldly affairs and lived out her existence as a nun in seclusion in Nishigamo, Kita Ward, Kyoto City.[147]

---

[146] "Shimabara, Kyoto." Wikipedia, Wikimedia Foundation, 26 Sept. 2023, en.wikipedia.org/wiki/Shimabara,_Kyoto.
[147] "桜木太夫 (Tayu Sakuragi)." Wikipedia, Wikimedia Foundation, 6 Nov. 2022, ja.wikipedia.org/wiki/%E6%A1%9C%E6%9C%A8%E5%A4%AA%E5%A4%AB.

xxxix. Ito Hirobumi as prime minister, circa the 1880s. Public domain.

Yugiri Dayu I

Yugiri Dayu, a renowned courtesan, had the extraordinary distinction of having worked in both the Shimabara and Shinmachi pleasure quarters of Kyoto and Osaka. She was among the three renowned tayu of her era, along with Yoshino Dayu and Takao Dayu.

Originally named Teru, she was born in Yamashiro Province, which is now known as Kyoto Prefecture. Yugiri was purchased by the Ogiya brothel in Shimabara and subsequently became the first tayu in Osaka in 1672, following the relocation of the brothel to Shinmachi. She adopted her name from the acclaimed Heian period novel, *The Tale of Genji*.

She reputedly excelled in the performing arts as a beautiful courtesan, but she died of illness six years after relocating to Shinmachi. She had only reached the age of 27. Her grave is located at Jokokuji Temple in Shimoteramachi, Osaka.

Her legacy encompasses the *Yugiri Memorial (Yugiri Festival)* and the *Flower Festival Yugiri Dayu Parade*, which takes place every year on the second Sunday of November as a tribute to her. Her life served as a profound source of inspiration for a multitude of compositions designed for the kabuki and *joruri* (Japanese puppet theater) stages in Japan.[148]

---

[148] "夕霧太夫 (Yugiri Dayu I)." Wikipedia, Wikimedia Foundation, 11 July 2021, ja.wikipedia.org/wiki/%E5%A4%95%E9%9C%A7%E5%A4%AA%E5%A4%AB.

Yachiyo Dayu

Yachiyo Dayu, whose given name was Takako, was born on June 15, 1635, and worked at the Shimabara pleasure quarter in Kyoto. She was born into the Hatano family in Himeji City, which was part of Harima Province, present-day Hyogo Prefecture.

She arrived at the Fukuda brothel, located in the Fushimi Chushojima district of Kyoto, at the age of eleven. In 1648, at the tender age of fourteen, she was elevated to the rank of *kakoi*, the second-highest rank of Kamigata courtesan, immediately below a tayu. Later, she moved to the Okumura brothel in Shimabara. She became a tayu on April 18, 1649, and took on the professional name Kodayu. She was only fifteen years old at the time. She assumed the name Yachiyo later in her career.

According to accounts, she was an exceptionally gifted individual. She excelled in multiple art forms including the shamisen, koto, kokyu, shakuhachi, kouta, sado, waka, haikai, and renga. Her calligraphy skills were so exceptional that she was acclaimed as the founder of her own calligraphy school.

In 1654, she extended an invitation to a lecturer hailing from the central region of Kyoto and commenced her study of Japanese literature. Her studies included renowned literary works such as *"Ise Monogatari"* ("The Tale of Ise"), *"Tsurezure gusa"* ("Essay in Idleness"), *"Kokin Wakashu"* ("A Collection of Ancient and Modern Japanese Poetry"), and *"Genji Monogatari"* ("The Tale of Genji"). Her lessons concluded in 1658 after the lecturer's health deteriorated.

Yachiyo also received recognition internationally. According to legend, the Chinese highly respected Yachiyo and skillfully stitched her emblem, which included a wreath of paulownia flowers, onto brocade fabric. This precious fabric was then sent to Nagasaki, Japan. Additionally, it is reported that during the Yi Dynasty in Korea, Yachiyo's crest was painted on porcelain after which it was shipped to Japan.

She departed the pleasure quarter on January 21, 1659, at the age of twenty-four. Her subsequent whereabouts and the time of her death remain unknown. Currently, a tayu, who has adopted the name Yachiyo, works at the Sumiya tea house in Kyoto. She engages in the art of tea ceremony and traditional Japanese dance.[149]

---

[149] Yu, A. C. "Yachiyo Tayu - Japanese Wiki Corpus." Yachiyo Tayu - Japanese Wiki Corpus, www.japanesewiki.com/person/Yachiyo%20tayu.html. Accessed 4 Jan. 2024.

*"I'd do it in the late morning, from 9 a.m.
It would go on until around 3 a.m. at night.
I cried and cried. It was really terrible.
I can never forget, even now, how awful it was. It was terrifying."*

*—1961 interview with an unnamed karayuki-san by author
Kohei Miyazaki (1917-1980)[150]*

---

[150] Author Kohei Miyazaki wanted to write a novel based on the lives of karayuki-san, but he later became busy with other work and died without completing the project. The tape was stored by his wife. The unnamed woman who had worked as a prostitute in Singapore since she was 16, and was 73 years old when the interview was conducted.

xl. Karayuki-san in Saigon, circa 1910. Public domain.

Karayuki

During the late 19th and early 20th centuries, Japanese girls and women who were trafficked to locations such as Manchuria, British India, East Asia, Southeast Asia, and Australia to work as prostitutes were referred to as *karayuki-san* (literally "Miss Gone to China" – the meaning later evolved during the Meiji era to mean "Miss Gone Abroad"). During this period, there was a network of Japanese prostitutes being trafficked across Asia, in what was then known as the "Yellow Slave Trade." Many of these women were the daughters of impoverished fishing or farming families, or were *burakumin* —ethnic Japanese descendants of pre-Meiji castes linked to *kegare* (defilement), including butchers, executioners, undertakers, slaughterhouse laborers, and tanners. The male and female mediators who facilitated the women's departures searched impoverished communities for young girls of suitable age and compensated their parents under the pretext that their daughters would be performing public service by traveling abroad. The mediators profited from selling the girls to individuals involved in the prostitution industry. Some mediators subsequently established brothels abroad using the funds they received.

China (especially Shanghai), Hong Kong, the Philippines, Indonesia (particularly Borneo and Sumatra), Thailand, and the western United States (mainly San Francisco) were among the primary destinations of the karayuki-san. They were often sent to Western colonies in Asia, where Chinese males and Western military personnel had ongoing needs for prostitutes. A market for karayuki-san was established by French soldiers as a consequence of the Sino-French War. As a result, prostitutes constituted the majority of the Japanese population in Indochina by 1908. There are documented instances of Japanese women who deployed to remote locations, which included Hawaii, Siberia, and Africa (Zanzibar). It was also possible to encounter Japanese prostitutes in both Bombay and Karachi.

In the Russian Far East, Japanese merchants and prostitutes comprised the majority of the Japanese population in the area after the 1860s. Japanese nationalist organizations such as the Amur River Society (*Kokuryukai*) and the Black Ocean Society (*Genyosha*) backed and aided the Japanese prostitutes stationed in the Russian Far East and Manchuria, even recruiting them as members. The prostitutes frequently assisted these organizations with espionage.

Japanese female trafficking overseas was facilitated by the absence of passport requirements for Japanese citizens at both Korean and Chinese ports. The smugglers transported these women under horrific conditions. Some girls were hidden in compartments below deck on the ships, and suffered from severe hunger or lack of oxygen. After surviving the crossing, the girls were trained in the practice of prostitution in cities including Kuala Lumpur, Hong Kong, or Singapore. Following their training, they were moved to different destinations.

The establishment of brothels in Singapore during the late 1890s was directly associated with the development of the Japanese enclave located at Middle Road. This community continued relying on prostitution as its primary economic activity for an extended period of time.

In 1910, a Japanese journalist detailed the living conditions of these workers in the *Fukuoka Nichinichi*, a local newspaper.

"Around nine o'clock, I went to see the infamous Malay Street. The buildings were constructed in a western style with their facades painted blue. Under the verandah hung red gas lanterns with numbers such as one, two or three, and wicker chairs were arranged beneath the lanterns. Hundreds and hundreds of young Japanese girls were sitting on the chairs calling out to passers-by, chatting and laughing... most of them were wearing yukata of striking colors... Most of them were young girls under 20 years of age. I learned from a maid at the hotel that the majority of these girls came from Shimabara and Amakusa in Kyushu."[151]

The Japanese government viewed the karayuki-led economic expansion into Southeast Asia as a deliberate strategy to develop a strong Japanese economic presence in the region. Profits from prostitution were utilized to bolster the growth of the Japanese economy and acquire more assets. Prostitutes served as both lenders and borrowers to other Japanese individuals. They used their earnings to provide financial support to Japanese tailors, physicians, and grocery stores. Additionally, they offered loans to other Japanese citizens who were trying to start their own businesses.

During the Russo-Japanese War, the estimated number of Japanese prostitutes in Singapore was around 700. However, due to the stoppage of European imports to Southeast Asia caused by World War I, Japanese products began replacing the items, leading to the Japanese community's shift toward retailing and trading as its economic basis.

After attaining the status of a Great Power, Japan's worldwide impact grew, resulting in improved circumstances and a transformation in the

---

[151] "Karayuki-San." Wikipedia, 23 Apr. 2023, en.wikipedia.org/wiki/Karayuki-san.

perception of karayuki-san, which started to be viewed as shameful. During the 1910s and 1920s, Japanese officials stationed overseas made significant endeavors, albeit not always achieving perfect success, to eliminate brothels and improve the reputation of Japan. Although the majority of karayuki-san repatriated to Japan, a small number chose to stay. Many courtesans endured miserable and isolated existences in exile, and sometimes succumbed to venereal diseases, neglect, and despair at young ages.

Following the Pacific War, the karayuki-san remained a relatively obscure aspect of Japan's concealed past. However, the release of the novel *Sandakan Brothel No. 8* by Tomoko Yamazaki in 1972 increased public knowledge of karayuki-san and prompted additional scholarly investigation and reporting.

Numerous films in Japanese popular culture portray the harsh working conditions endured by the karayuki-san. The following films were shot entirely or in part on location: *Karayuki-san* (1937, Toho Studios), *The Blossoming Port* (1943, Shochiku Studios), and *Whoremonger* (1987, Toei Studios). The film adaptation of Tomoko Yamazaki's novel *Sandakan No. 8* was released in 1974, directed by Kei Kumai. Kohei Miyazaki's *Shimabara Lullaby* was released in the same year, and *Karayuki-san, the Making of a Prostitute* was released in 1975.

Furthermore, numerous publications have been produced on this subject. *The Memoir of Keiko Karayuki-san in Siam* explores the ordeals of Japanese young women who were coerced into engaging in prostitution in Thailand. *Ah Ku and Karayuki-san: Prostitution in Singapore, 1870-*

1940 provides a comprehensive analysis of the karayuki-san phenomenon in Singapore throughout the specified time period.[152]

---

[152] "Karayuki-San." Wikipedia.

Yamada Waka

xli. *Yamada Waka and her husband, Kakichi, Public domain.*

Yamada Waka née Asaba (December 1, 1879–September 6, 1957), was active during the late Meiji, Taisho, and Showa periods of Japan, and was a pioneering Japanese feminist and social reformer.

She was born into an impoverished peasant family in present-day Kanagawa Prefecture. In 1897, at the age of 18, she relocated to Yokohama in search of employment. She was abducted and taken to Seattle, in the United States, where she was coerced into engaging in prostitution using the pseudonym "Arabian Oyae." She was held there as a sex slave until 1900, when she met Shinzaburo Ritsui, a Japanese journalist who helped her escape to San Francisco after becoming captivated by her story. However, her "savior" also sexually exploited her. Waka fled and encountered Cameron House, a Presbyterian ministry established to assist prostitutes in breaking free from their oppressors. Waka became a Christian and began working at the mission while learning English. In 1903, she met Yamada Kakichi, a sociologist who operated an English language school. They fell in love and married the following year, and in 1906 they moved back to Japan.

After moving to the Yotsuya Ward in Tokyo, Waka discovered the literary works of Ellen Key, a prominent Swedish champion of women's rights who focused extensively on the government's role in safeguarding motherhood, pregnancy, childbirth, and childcare. In addition, Waka's husband began teaching foreign languages to Osugi Sakae, a Japanese anarchist, who then introduced Waka to Hiratsuka Raicho's magazine, *Bluestocking* (*Seito*). Later, Waka began a career dedicated to advocating for women's rights.

Her frequent contributions to *Bluestocking* solidified Waka's position as a figure of enormous significance in the Japanese women's movement. Notwithstanding her society's disapproval, she openly revealed her personal experiences as a prostitute and provided a detailed account of the mistreatment she had endured. The Japanese newspaper, *Asahi Shimbun*, featured her in a recurring women's column.

Unlike many other Japanese feminists of her era, she primarily dedicated herself to protecting and promoting the dignity of the traditional feminine roles of wife and mother. This ambition mirrored the objectives of Ellen Key, whose ideas served as an ideological inspiration for her. It also coincided with the viewpoints of Imperial Japan, which advocated for the importance of virtuous mothers and obedient wives. Waka's position created a sharp division between her and contemporary feminists, who were against Japan's imperial aspirations and promoted gender equality with less focus on domestic and maternal duties.

Waka advocated for a "Mother and Child Protection Act", which culminated in the founding of the New Women's Association (*Shin Fujin Kyokai*). In 1934, she founded the Women's League (soon renamed the Maternity Protection League (*Bosei Hogo Renmei*) and became its chair.

Because of her distinguished standing, Waka received an invitation to meet Eleanor Roosevelt at the White House on December 7, 1937, while she was on a lecture tour of the United States. In 1938, she founded the first refuge in Japan dedicated to providing shelter for children and women seeking safety from abusive situations.

Waka was deeply troubled by the implementation of government-sanctioned prostitution for American military personnel stationed in Japan following the conclusion of World War II. Despite the quick closure of state-supported brothels, a significant number of prostitutes continued to operate on the streets during the tumultuous postwar era. Many of these women had lost their homes and families in the conflict.

Waka founded a comparable educational establishment to Cameron House in Tokyo in 1947, with the intention of providing practical skills to Japanese prostitutes so they could find other employment and support themselves.[153]

---

[153] "Yamada Waka." Wikipedia, 11 June 2023, en.wikipedia.org/wiki/Yamada_Waka.

Orandayuki

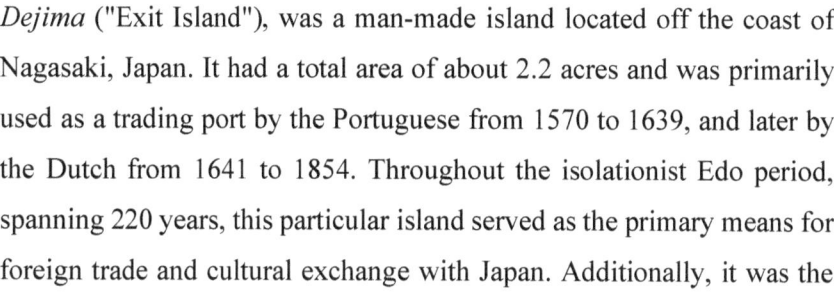

Dejima ("Exit Island"), was a man-made island located off the coast of Nagasaki, Japan. It had a total area of about 2.2 acres and was primarily used as a trading port by the Portuguese from 1570 to 1639, and later by the Dutch from 1641 to 1854. Throughout the isolationist Edo period, spanning 220 years, this particular island served as the primary means for foreign trade and cultural exchange with Japan. Additionally, it was the only area in Japan accessible to Westerners.

After the expulsion of the Portuguese in 1639 due to their suspected role in a Christian revolt called the Shimabara Uprising in 1637, Dejima had a decrease in commercial activity, causing a significant economic downturn for Nagasaki. As a result, government officials exerted pressure on the Dutch to relocate from Hirado to Dejima. The Dutch had arrived in Bungo, Oita Prefecture, in 1600 and later set up a trading post at Hirado. The Dutch maintained favor by supplying gunpowder and cannons to the shogunate to suppress the insurrection, earning them exclusive commercial privileges in Japan. [154] Dejima comprised residences for approximately twenty Dutch nationals, warehouses, and accommodations for Japanese government officials. A team of Japanese officials, guards, night watchmen, and a supervisor with over fifty subordinates closely monitored the Dutch.

Beginning in 1641, the privilege of entering Japan was restricted to Chinese and Dutch ships, and they were only allowed to dock in Nagasaki

---

[154] "Dejima: Nagasaki's 400-Year-Old Dutch Trading Post." Japanistry.Com, 13 Oct. 2021, www.japanistry.com/dejima/.

harbor. Each vessel that arrived in Dejima underwent inspection. The Japanese confiscated the ship's sails until they allowed it to depart. Although the Dutch faced significant financial challenges in sustaining the remote colony on Dejima, their trade with Japan proved highly lucrative.[155]

Only authorized sex workers were permitted to enter the island, and no other ladies were allowed. The sex workers, referred to as *orandayuki* ("Miss Gone to Holland"), were an exceptionally cultured and refined group. They seamlessly incorporated Dutch and Malay vocabulary into their discourse while they engaged in a sincere exchange of kisses and handshakes. They utilized umbrellas of Western origin, adorned themselves with bracelets and rings embellished with valuable gemstones, consumed coffee, and indulged in chocolate. In addition, they engaged in a game of billiards, known as *tamatsuki,* with the Dutch.

Similar to the karayuki, who were granted permission to serve Japanese customers but were prohibited from entering the Dutch ward, the orandayuki were authorized to cater to Japanese clients but were prevented from entering the Chinese ward. The Nagasaki magistrates had raised concerns that allowing the prostitutes to frequent both neighborhoods might facilitate the smuggling of cash and messages between the Dutch and the Chinese. Nevertheless, this strategy was shown to be ineffectual in thwarting the illicit transmission of messages and financial transactions between foreign individuals and local residents seeking to engage with them. The courtesans also participated in petty smuggling for personal profit, with the intention of selling their

---

[155] "Dejima." Wikipedia, Wikimedia Foundation, 12 Nov. 2023, en.wikipedia.org/wiki/Dejima.

merchandise on the black market. They discreetly hid small objects beneath their kimono robes and wrapped imported silk fabric tightly under their obi belts.[156]

Due to the significantly greater fees charged to Dutch customers compared to Chinese and Japanese clients, as well as the Dutch tendency to give extravagant gifts, some young women formed romantic relationships with the Dutch. As such, during the first half of the eighteenth century, there was a steady rise in the population of *nazuke-yujo* or *shikiri-yujo*. These terms refer to prostitutes who were not formally sold to brothels, but rather voluntarily registered themselves as prostitutes for personal, mainly economic, reasons. In fact, the number of these unregistered prostitutes grew to such an extent that in 1754 and 1759, steps were taken to prohibit their entry into Dejima.[157]

---

[156] Stanley, Amy. "Regulation and the Logic of the Household." *Selling Women: Prostitution, Markets, and the Household in Early Modern Japan,* University of California Press, Berkeley, 2012, p. 80.
[157] "Forgotten Foibles: Love and the Dutch at Dejima (1641–1854)."

xlii. Portrait of Kusumoto Ine's mother, Kusumoto Taki, circa the 1830s. Public domain.

xliii. Philipp Franz Balthasar von Siebold. Public domain.

Kusumoto Taki

The poverty that resulted from famine and agricultural failures increased the chances for Japanese men to fulfill their sexual urges and turned Japan into a destination for foreign men seeking sexual satisfaction. Parents would rent their unmarried daughters to foreign sailors for a few weeks or several months. Occasionally, these ladies married the foreign men they had sexual intercourse with or became their long-term concubines.

Kusumoto Ine (1827–1903), originally named Shiimoto Ine, held the distinction of being Japan's pioneering female practitioner of Western medicine. She was the daughter of German physician Philipp Franz Balthasar von Siebold, who conducted medical research on Dejima, and Nagasaki courtesan Kusumoto Taki. In 1823, at the age of sixteen, Kusumoto Taki was sent from the Maruyama pleasure quarter in Nagasaki to become Siebold's concubine.

On October 22, 1829, Siebold was exiled on suspicion of illicitly exporting restricted materials that he had obtained from the geographer Takahashi Kageyasu. Japanese authorities believed that Siebold unlawfully smuggled maps of Japan, which could have been intercepted by Japan's adversaries and endangered Japan's northern borders. Prior to his exile, Ine had lived with her parents on Dejima.

Taki and Ine, who was two years old at the time, were denied authorization to leave Japan. As Siebold's vessel set sail, his family waved goodbye to him from a tiny boat in the harbor. Later, Taki married a Japanese man named Wasaburo.

Ine was also referred to as O-Ine and later adopted the name Itoku. Due to her association with Dejima and its Dutch-language Western education, she is commonly known as Oranda O-Ine ("Dutch O-Ine") in Japanese.

Siebold, a wealthy individual, left Taki and Ine a generous amount of valuable sugar to guarantee their survival. In addition, he arranged for his colleagues to watch over them. His students made valuable contributions to Ine's education, and Siebold provided her with books on Dutch grammar that played a pivotal role in advancing Western studies in Japan during that period.

According to a dubious legend, Ine escaped to Uwajima Domain at the age of 14 or 15 to pursue the study of medicine under the tutelage of Ninomiya Keisaku, who had been placed under house arrest for his involvement in the Siebold Affair.

Ine's status was elevated once she received accreditation as a Western medicine practitioner, thanks to the support of feudal lord Date Munenari. She received instruction in different regions of Japan from multiple tutors, one of whom fathered her child, most likely through non-consensual means, leading to the birth of her only daughter. She remained unmarried throughout her life. In 1873, she aided one of Emperor Meiji's concubines as she gave birth. When Japan ended its isolation from other nations, she relocated to Tokyo. Since her death, Ine has been held in high regard in Japan and has inspired a vast array of artistic works, including musicals, plays, novels, and manga.[158]

---

[158] "Kusumoto Ine." Wikipedia, 13 Sept. 2021, en.wikipedia.org/wiki/Kusumoto_Ine.

xliv. Photo of Kusumoto Ine. Public domain.

Jigoku Dayu: Hell Courtesan

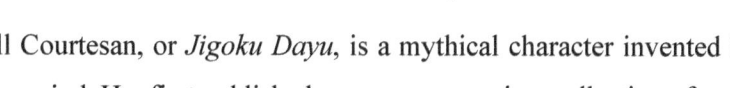

Hell Courtesan, or *Jigoku Dayu*, is a mythical character invented in the Edo period. Her first published appearance was in a collection of comedic short stories released anonymously in 1672.

Jigoku Dayu, as legend holds, was the daughter of a samurai. She was originally named Otoboshi. After her father died in combat while she was still young, her family moved out of their home. However, they encountered outlaws while fleeing. She and her elder sister were sold when their mother was murdered. After some time, Otoboshi ended up at a brothel in Sakai, Osaka Prefecture. There she attained the rank of tayu.

Otoboshi came to believe that her present predicament was retribution for wrongdoings committed in a prior life. She hoped to carry out a form of penance by adopting the name *Jigoku* (Hell) and having representative images of hell embroidered on her kimono.[159] She eventually became associated with the eccentric and iconoclastic Zen Buddhist monk and poet Ikkyu. Ikkyu, who lived from 1394 to 1481, was a real person, in contrast to the legendary Jigoku.

Ikkyu was born in a small suburb of Kyoto. He is commonly believed to have been the son of Emperor Go-Komatsu (the 100th emperor of Japan) and a low-ranking court noblewoman. At the age of thirteen, Ikkyu entered Kennin-ji temple in Kyoto to study Zen under the tutelage of the renowned priest Botetsu. Here, he began composing poetry. At times,

---

[159] Matsuura, Thersa. "Jigoku Tayuu: The Mysterious Hell Courtesan (Ep. 74)." Uncanny Japan Podcast, 15 Apr. 2021, uncannyjapan.com/podcast/jigoku-tayuu/.

Ikkyu was considered a troublemaker. He often irritated his teacher with his remarks and actions toward guests, and he was known for his heavy drinking. He cultivated an inner circle of eminent poets and artists and developed an intimate connection with Mori, a blind singer who later became his life partner.

He was one of a handful of Zen priests who, within a religious context, addressed the topic of sexuality, including sex with prostitutes, monastic homosexuality, and lovers, on the grounds that such activities promoted enlightenment. Sex, in his opinion, was an inherent aspect of human nature and, as such, more virtuous than hypocritical organizations and secular pursuits.[160]

Fascinated by Jigoku's notoriety, Ikkyu decided to visit her at the brothel. However, when presented to the impoverished and disheveled monk, the brothel owner refused to allow him inside. As a consequence, Ikkyu's behavior became unbearable, leading to his removal and the possibility of being physically assaulted. It is alleged that Jigoku Dayu intervened and extended him an invitation to enter.

Despite the established practice of monks abstaining from meat and alcohol, Ikkyu specifically requested a portion of carp, sake, and steaming hot broth. After obtaining his order, he proceeded to become extremely intoxicated. Following this, Jigoku developed a suspicion that Ikkyu was not, in fact, a renowned monk, but rather was acting dishonestly. She thought it would be fair to give him one last test before showing him the door.

Unbeknownst to him, she dispatched a group of musicians and dancers to his room and secretly observed him from behind a paper screen. Ikkyu was ecstatic, so he joyfully rose to his feet and began dancing with them.

---

[160] "Ikkyū." Wikipedia, Wikimedia Foundation, 17 Dec. 2023, en.wikipedia.org/wiki/Ikky%C5%AB.

Jigoku began to depart in dismay, but she stopped upon noticing the peculiar configuration of the shadows on the paper screen. Upon further inspection, she noticed that the entire ensemble of musicians and dancers had transformed into skeletal figures. At that instant, she came to the realization that death is perpetually present beneath the allure and appeal of life. Every one of us must face death eventually. Subsequently, she commenced her Buddhist studies under the guidance of Ikkyu, who imparted teachings on impermanence and other related principles.

The teacher and disciple had a long-lasting and continuous friendship. According to certain accounts, Jigoku indicated a wish to renounce her profession and embark on a path as a female monk, but Ikkyu discouraged her from doing so.

Jigoku fell very ill. On the 45th day of her illness, she predicted her impending death and called for Ikkyu. Upon his arrival, Jigoku summoned her last bit of strength to skillfully play the koto and sing. Upon finishing the song, she promptly collapsed and died. Ikkyu instructed her attendants to dress her in a simple white kimono and abandon her in the fields. They expressed their disapproval; however, one of Ikkyu's followers uncovered a message beneath Jigoku's pillow confirming her true intention. As a final act of benevolence, Jigoku requested that she be left in the field to serve as food for the starving dogs.[161]

---

[161] Matsuura, Thersa. "Jigoku Tayuu: The Mysterious Hell Courtesan (Ep. 74)."

xlv. Hell Courtesan (Jigoku Dayû) by Kawanabe Kyōsa,i circa 1870-1880s. Public domain.

"The boys seen as ideal partners for danshoku affairs had not yet gone through their genpuku coming-of-age ceremony, and were considered to be beautiful as girls; relationships were expected to last for just a few years while they were in their mid-teens. As vulnerable members of a society of self-centered men, the boys would often be discarded, and in extreme cases might be killed after their genpuku."

— Saeki Junko, "Male-Male Desire: 'Danshoku' Culture and Its Legacy in Japan," Nippon.com, Sep 29, 2023.

xlvi. Samurai and Male Youth by Miyagawa Issho, early 18th century. Public domain

Kagema: The Male Sex Workers

There is a widely held idea on the origins of homosexuality (*nanshoku*, which can also be read as *danshoku*) in Japan, which proposes that the Buddhist monk Kukai, also known as Kobo Daishi after his passing, introduced this custom in 806 CE following his return from China. This is a commonly accepted "origin story." However, its veracity cannot be substantiated.

Whether or not the myth surrounding the origins of homosexuality in Japan is true, these relationships were common, particularly in Buddhist monasteries where *chigo*, or apprentices, were present. During the medieval era, the chigo would groom themselves by shaving their eyebrows, applying powder on their faces, and dressing in women's attire. These actions were driven by two motives. First, the chigo served as a representation of aesthetic appeal in both everyday life and sacred rituals. Additionally, they fulfilled the role of attendants and often participated in amorous relationships with the elder monks.

Homosexual behaviors with young boys were not exclusive to Buddhist monks. In Shintoism, Japan's other prevailing religion, there is no condemnation of same-sex relationships between males. In fact, Shintoism embraces sexuality in general as a natural and inherent aspect of life. Due to the lack of condemnation of homosexual activity in Shintoism, Japanese Shinto priests were able to engage in intimacy with young boys without repercussions. Due to their social exclusion and disdain for women, these priests turned to *bido*, or beautiful boys, as a way to satiate their lust without having to deal with the negative effects of becoming a father or becoming emotionally involved for an extended length of time. They maintained that their vows of celibacy remained unbroken even after engaging in sexual activity with a chigo, as they believed that male sexual contact did not meet the criteria for actual intercourse.

Prostitution was legal and gained greater social acceptance during the Edo period, which also led to the rise in the popularity of services catering to homosexual male clientele. Until 1956, Shinjuku's Ni-chome was recognized as one of Tokyo's unofficial red-light districts. Initially, it was a pleasure quarter where female prostitutes were commercially exploited, but subsequently it transformed into a sanctuary for homosexual men. Today, it is still a buzzing, neon-lit gay quarter in East Shinjuku.

Toward the end of the medieval period and into the Edo period, male priests represented a significant demographic of customers for the young male sex workers known as *kagema*. Frequently, brothels catering to homosexuals were located in close proximity to Buddhist temples, granting priests convenient access. During the Edo period, the clientele expanded to include members of the samurai class as well as the highest strata of society.

The samurai, despite their elevated status, were ordinary men who experienced human wants that could only be fulfilled by companionship with another individual. Spending most of their time with other men, their options were often limited. Homosexuality was commonly acknowledged as an integral aspect of a soldier's identity. The well-known proverb,

"*Nanshoku wa bumon no hana* (Nanshoku is the flower of the military class)," exemplified this cultural practice.[162]

The *kagema* served a diverse clientele consisting of both men and women, although the male clientele comprised the majority. They often posed as apprentice kabuki actors who frequently performed sex work on the side. Kagema that were not affiliated with an official kabuki theater were available for hire through male brothels or teahouses specializing in kagema. These establishments were referred to as *kagemajaya*, which literally translates to "kagema teahouse." [163]

By the late 17th century, male brothels had emerged not just in major urban centers, but also in large rural communities, rest stops, and small temple-towns.

If an actor or a tea house employee achieved significant popularity, both they and the *kagemajaya* proprietor could generate substantial financial gains. Occasionally, a customer desired to demonstrate their discernment and refinement by spending a significant sum of money on a certain boy. At other times, a customer simply wished to win the boy's services over other clients. Women were able to rent boys as well. During the Edo period, it was not difficult for women to obtain pornography, sex devices, or the services of both male and female prostitutes, despite the considerable social stigma associated with such activities. During the height of teahouse prosperity, the smug young bourgeois indolent emerged as the archetypal patron, irresponsibly spending his allowance

---

[162] Edwards, Meradeth Lin. *Professional Heartbreakers: Male Entertainers and the Divide Between Popular Culture and History in Japan*. University of San Diego - Digital USD, 2018, digital.sandiego.edu/cgi/viewcontent.cgi?article=1030&context=theses.
[163] "Kagema." Wikipedia, Wikimedia Foundation, 29 Apr. 2023, en.wikipedia.org/wiki/Kagema.

(or inheritance) on an extensive number of prostitutes. These customers would enter a teahouse and select a boy of their choosing. Numerous teahouses compiled employee rosters that included some form of information catering to the diverse preferences of their patrons. The following list from a *kagemajaya* in the Dotonbori neighborhood of Osaka is one such example:

Hanayama Tounosuke (14)	Fair complexion, lovely eyes, recites kodaya tunes.
Iwataki Isaburou (16)	Skillful dancer, sings nage tunes, naturally imitates the manners of a woman.
Yumekawa Dairoku (15)	Good drinker, who can keep up with anyone. Plays shamisen well, and is the most attractive of those dressed like traveling performers.
Matsunokaze Kotonojou (17)	Good at making shadow figures, and can spit water from his mouth to write characters on the wall. In juggling, he rivals Shio no Choujirou.
Fukakusa Kankyuurou (17)	In his manner of speaking, he closely resembles the late Suzuki Heihachi [actor]. He has no special skills but is wonderful in bed![164]

---

[164] Edwards, Meradeth Lin. "Professional Heartbreakers: Male Entertainers and the Divide Between Popular Culture and History in Japan.

After the decision had been reached, the client accompanied his selected boy into a room. The fees were proportional to the boy's status, mirroring the structure of the courtesans in brothels.[165]

Throughout the mid-19th century, kagema maintained a thriving trade and charged higher rates than female sex workers of comparable status. This continued despite the implementation of stricter legal regulations that sought to confine sex workers, male and female, to particular urban areas and discourage class-spanning relationships, which were perceived as potentially disruptive, to established social structures.

Like the female sex workers, many young kabuki actors and kagema, aged eight and up, were typically sold to theaters and brothels as indentured servants on ten-year contracts.[166] When the practice of selling off girls was no longer sufficient, a desperate family might resort to offering their sons either for training as actors or for sale to teahouse proprietors. These males, as opposed to the female children who were required to serve as kamuro until they attained the necessary age, were commonly trained and employed as sex workers at an extremely young age. To maintain the favor of their male clientele, young male prostitutes would do anything to prolong their youth. As time passed, their clientele tended to transition from males to females as they aged and developed into adults.

Although male prostitution was well-established in theater areas, it was not officially recognized or subject to taxation like female prostitution. In the mid-1800s, male tea houses experienced a decrease in popularity as

---

[165] Edwards, Meradeth Lin. Professional Heartbreakers: Male Entertainers and the Divide Between Popular Culture and History in Japan.
[166] "Kagema." Wikipedia.

female brothels gained prominence. During the Tenpo era (1830-1843), characterized by reforms that prioritized thriftiness in both governmental and personal matters, and censored indecent works of art and literature, there were only two tea houses with ten boys remaining in the town of Yoshicho. The Meiji Restoration inflicted significant damage to the male prostitution industry by dispersing priest communities, thereby greatly reducing the number of potential customers.[167]

---

[167] Edwards, Meradeth Lin. Professional Heartbreakers: Male Entertainers and the Divide Between Popular Culture and History in Japan.

Prostitution During the Meiji Period and Beyond

The term *baishun okoku* (kingdom of whoring) was used to describe Japan during the Meiji Period.[168] Japan had around 350 officially sanctioned red-light districts and 150 unsanctioned red-light districts that were active during this period. Consequently, missionaries and diplomats, including Rutherford Alcock (1809-1897), the first British diplomatic representative to establish residence in Japan, leveled severe criticism on the country. Nevertheless, geisha and prostitutes were bound by contracts of indentured servitude until the *Prostitute Emancipation Act* (*Geishōgi kaihō rei*) was enacted by the Meiji government in 1872. Despite initially appearing as a forward-thinking and beneficial measure, it ultimately led to a significant number of women becoming jobless and lacking alternative means of support. As a result, some brothels opted to rebrand themselves as *kashizashiki gyo* or room rental establishments, attracting a substantial number of women to work under similar agreements, even though they were no longer explicitly referred to as prostitutes. Within a span of only three years, the government altered its stance and reinstated the legality of indenture contracts involving prostitutes.[169]

Shortly thereafter, a Japanese Protestant missionary and educator, Niijima Jo, better known by his English name, Joseph Hardy Neesima, launched a movement against the licensing of red-light districts. Soon, others

---

[168] "Prostitution in Japan." Wikipedia, Wikimedia Foundation.
[169] 遊女 (Yujo)." Wikipedia, Wikimedia Foundation, 15 Aug. 2023, ja.wikipedia.org/wiki/%E9%81%8A%E5%A5%B3.

joined him and newspapers began referring to prostitutes as "ugly women." In the end, changing public opinion contributed to the decline in the social status of geisha and courtesans.[170]

In 1900, the *Shogi torishimari kisoku* (Ordinance No. 44) was promulgated by the Japanese government, introducing limitations on the working conditions within the prostitution industry. Only those who possessed parental consent, were unmarried, and at least 18 years old were eligible to work as government-licensed prostitutes. The restriction failed to decrease the general prevalence of prostitution and did not provide women with greater freedom. On the contrary, prostitution thrived throughout the Meiji period. According to a survey conducted at the end of 1904, the country was host to over 42,000 government-licensed prostitutes and 26,000 geisha.[171]

Soon after, additional legislation was enacted. The purpose of implementing Article 16 was to require the registration of prostitutes on the prostitute register and to restrict their activities to specific room rental establishments. Due to these stipulations, the government was able to lawfully impose taxes on prostitution. Hence, it is reasonable to infer that the primary aim of the legislation was to generate revenue for the government rather than to promote the cause of human rights or freedom. In fact, during the late Tokugawa and early Meiji periods, the prostitution industry provided a substantial portion of the government's revenue.[172]

During the Taisho Period (1912–1926), registered sex workers were permitted to operate in room rental establishments situated in six

---

[170] 遊女 (Yujo)." Wikipedia, Wikimedia Foundation.
[171] "Prostitution in Japan." Wikipedia, Wikimedia Foundation.
[172] "Prostitution in Japan." Wikipedia, Wikimedia Foundation.

designated areas of Tokyo. The aforementioned locations were Yoshiwara, Suzaki, Shinjuku, Shinagawa, Senju, and Itabashi. In 1921, Tokyo had a total of 5,600 registered prostitutes. More than 80% of the sex workers operated in Yoshiwara, Suzaki, and Shinjuku, drawing in over 300,000 clients in just six months.

In the 1930s, more than 20 countries globally had regulated systems for prostitution. However, Japan was the only country to implement legislation that imposed limitations on the freedom of movement for prostitutes. The Johnson Committee of the League of Nations denounced the system as both inhumane and antiquated. The ban on leaving, as specified in Article 7 of the *Regulations for the Control of Prostitutes*, was lifted in 1933.

Numerous young women were conscripted by the government during the Sino-Japanese War (1937-1945) under the *Military Service Law*, approved by the Imperial Diet. These women were deployed as comfort women, offering sexual services to soldiers and civilians in territories under Japanese rule, such as China, Manchuria, and Southeast Asia.

During the Allied occupation of Japan that followed World War II, prostitution was confined to the *akasen*, or red-line zones, which were areas historically linked to the sex work industry. This restriction was in accordance with a 1946 GHQ directive.[173]

---

[173] "遊女 (Yujo)." Wikipedia, Wikimedia Foundation, 15 Aug. 2023, ja.wikipedia.org/wiki/%E9%81%8A%E5%A5%B3.

xlvii. Yasuura House (Recreation and Amusement Association) brothel in Yokosuka City, circa 1945-46, public domain

Sex During the Occupation: The RAA

The Recreation and Amusement Association (RAA), also known as the Special Comfort Facility Association, was the largest organization created by Japanese authorities after World War II. Its objective was to provide organized prostitution as a deterrent against sexual assaults and violence committed against the local female population by Allied occupation forces. In addition, the RAA sought to create diverse recreational facilities for the Allied forces stationed in the area.[174]

---

[174] Recreation and Amusement Association." Wikipedia, 22 Mar. 2023, en.wikipedia.org/wiki/Recreation_and_Amusement_Association.

Japanese authorities established the RAA on August 21, 1945, to cater to the needs of Allied occupation troops. Before its establishment, the Home Ministry had issued an order to prefectural governors and police chiefs on August 18, urging them to make appropriate preparations for creating "comfort facilities" in districts where the Allied occupation forces were expected to be stationed. These establishments, comprising dance halls, restaurants, taverns, and brothels, were designed to be staffed by women already engaged in the sex industry. However, given the scarcity of women in the industry and the widespread issue of women facing food shortages, the recruitment process was expanded by placing newspaper ads that concealed the true nature of the work, while promising provisions such as food, clothing, and shelter. Government officials utilized nationalistic rhetoric to present the comfort facility system, commending the women who voluntarily served as "patriotic barriers" to protect Japanese women and girls from sexual abuse. It is estimated that during World War II, Allied military forces committed sexual assault against approximately 10,000 women in Okinawa.[175] The Japanese authorities believed that the establishment of brothels might decrease instances of sexual violence perpetrated by the Allied occupation forces.

Unlike other regions in the country, the Tokyo area adopted a unique approach in response to the expected large number of foreign personnel being stationed there. In a conference with the leaders of the Tokyo Restaurant Association, the Superintendent-General of the Metropolitan Police Headquarters requested their assistance in coordinating preparations for the impending troops' arrival. The leaders of the Tokyo Restaurant Association utilized their connections to assemble a

---

[175] Recreation and Amusement Association." Wikipedia.

consortium of delegates from the nightclub, bar, and brothel industries. These delegates met with the law enforcement authorities during which time they were officially requested to create "comfort facilities" while minimizing the visibility of the government's involvement. These individuals formed the "Special Comfort Facilities Association" (later renamed the Recreation and Amusement Association) two days later. Ahead of schedule, Hayato Ikeda, the director of the Tax Bureau of the Ministry of Finance, facilitated unsecured loans provided by the Japan Industrial Development Bank to the organization. The 33-million-yen loan that the RAA obtained was distributed among its members.

The first brothel, named Komachien Garden, opened for business on September 20, 1945, with a staff of 150 women. By December 1945, the RAA possessed a total of 34 establishments, with 16 of them specifically designated as "comfort stations."[176] As previously pointed out, the initial objective was for the ladies hired at the comfort facilities to be persons with prior experience in the sex industry. In reality, there was an enormous shortage of prostitutes, particularly in the Tokyo region. The government had cracked down on prostitution late in the war, and many women had fled or been evacuated to the countryside following heavy Allied bombing of strategic centers and residential areas. Yoshiwara, Tokyo's renowned red-light district, had experienced a drastic decline in its number of prostitutes from 2,000 before the war to just a few dozen by the war's end.[177] Hence, it was inevitable that efforts were undertaken to enlist individuals from the overall populace, a strategy that was sanctioned by the law enforcement authorities. Alongside the prostitutes,

---

[176] Recreation and Amusement Association." Wikipedia.
[177] Recreation and Amusement Association." Wikipedia.

the RAA also recruited a substantial number of "dancers" who received payment for dancing with soldiers. However, the line between the terms "dancer" and "prostitute" gradually became blurred.

Women were recruited extensively through independent brokers. These brokers, a significant number of whom were associated with the *yakuza* (members of organized crime syndicates), employed morally questionable methods for recruiting. The Women's Volunteer Corps, a government organization for mobilizing girls and women aged 14–25 for work in factories, was a popular target as many of these women were left unemployed and stranded by the end of the war.

Despite these deceptive recruitment practices, most women working in the comfort stations ultimately consented to work as prostitutes. Furthermore, some women were unable to leave the brothels because they had been sold by their impoverished families or were in debt to the establishment. Certain comfort stations employed manipulative strategies such as "company store" methods and provided loan advances that trapped women in a cycle of debt that prevented them from leaving.

The practice of obligating women to work in brothels as a means of repaying debts was ultimately prohibited through a Supreme Commander for the Allied Powers directive (SCAPIN 642) in January 1946. However, several Japanese authorities expressed doubts about the effectiveness of enforcing such a prohibition.

When utilizing the RAA brothels, GIs were issued a ticket priced at 100 yen (equal to $0.70 in 2023) upon arrival, which was handed to the ladies who serviced them. Every day, the women, who typically served 15 to 60 clients, would bring the tickets to the station's accounting office in the morning and collect 50 yen for each ticket.[178]

Female personnel in many RAA facilities experienced frequent occurrences of sexual violence similar to those observed in the sex trade. Female dancers were particularly susceptible to rape. In addition, military police and GIs occasionally requested free service or refunds. The power disparity between Japanese police and Allied soldiers posed a significant obstacle for the women to voice their grievances.

On October 14, the Japanese police removed its restrictions on brothels and night clubs, effectively approving the non-RAA sex industry that catered to Occupation troops. As a result, 25 non-RAA comfort stations employing 1,500 women cropped up in Tokyo by the end of November.[179]

American medical officers established prophylactic stations in red-light districts and inside the larger brothels; that distributed tens of thousands of condoms each week. Despite these precautions, sexually transmitted diseases, primarily gonorrhea and syphilis, became a serious public health issue. By the beginning of 1946, an estimated 25% of all US occupation personnel were afflicted, with several units seeing infection rates of nearly 50 percent.[180] In response, the GHQ implemented rigorous processes to screen prostitutes for sexually transmitted diseases, designated specific brothels with high infection rates as prohibited for troops, and assisted in the re-establishment of clinics and laboratories (many of which were destroyed during the war) to diagnose illnesses. Moreover, the 8th Army granted permission for the unrestricted

---

[178] Recreation and Amusement Association." Wikipedia.
[179] Recreation and Amusement Association." Wikipedia.
[180] Recreation and Amusement Association." Wikipedia.

distribution of penicillin to afflicted prostitutes, even though there was an alarming shortage of the drug in the United States—and despite instructions from Washington that it should only be administered to Japanese individuals "as a life saving measure."

Not all those in the occupation forces accepted the widespread patronizing of Japanese-sanctioned brothels by U.S. troops. Some unit commanders considered prostitution an "endemic problem that plagued their troops" and tried, with limited success, to prevent their men from fraternizing with the Japanese. In the beginning of 1946, military chaplains expressed strong disapproval of SCAP's leniency, pointing out the infringement of War Department regulations and the detrimental impact it had on the moral standards of U.S. troops.

During its peak, the RAA employed around 55,000 women, the majority of whom were involved in prostitution.[181] However, just seven months after their establishment, RAA brothels were officially declared off-limits to prevent the spread of sexually transmitted diseases. They were subsequently placed under official shutdown.

The immediate consequence of the cessation of legalized brothel prostitution was the abrupt joblessness of numerous women. A significant number of them resorted to engaging in street prostitution as "panpan" prostitutes.

The proliferation of street prostitution posed challenges for GHQ. It could not effectively manage the spread of sexually transmitted diseases, and this contributed to a surge in sexual assaults perpetrated by GIs. Prior to

---

[181] Recreation and Amusement Association." Wikipedia.

the closing down of the RAA brothels, the average number of women involved in such incidents was 40 per day, but this figure skyrocketed to an estimated 330 per day immediately following the shutdown.[182]

In November 1946, the Japanese government implemented the *akasen* (red-line) system, allowing prostitution in specific authorized zones.[183] Another name, *aosen* (blue-line), referred to sex industry districts that were neither permitted or lawful.

---

[182] Recreation and Amusement Association." Wikipedia.
[183] "Recreation and Amusement Association." Wikipedia, 22 Mar. 2023, en.wikipedia.org/wiki/Recreation_and_Amusement_Association.

xlviii. Jan Ruff O'Herne (Bandoengan, Java, 1942), public domain

The Comfort Women

Comfort women were women and girls who were coerced into sexual servitude by the Imperial Japanese Army in countries and territories under Japanese occupation prior to and during World War II. The term "comfort women" is a direct translation of the Japanese word *ianfu*, which carries the literal meaning of "woman providing comfort and solace." During World War II, Japanese forces pressed a large number of women from several nations, including Australia, Burma, China, Netherlands, Philippines, Japan, Korea, Indonesia, and others, into sexual slavery for the benefit of Japanese troops. It is worth noting that the majority of these women were from Korea. A significant number of women perished or took their own lives as a result of severe abuse and enduring bodily and psychological anguish.

Following the war, Japan's recognition of the suffering endured by the comfort women was insufficient, as it lacked a complete apology and proper compensation. This failure had a detrimental impact on Japan's standing in Asia for many years. The Japanese government did not officially apologize and offer compensation until the 1990s.

The number of women who were involved in sexual servitude is subject to varying estimates, with the majority of historians approximating it to be between 50,000 and 200,000.[184] Few records exist regarding the enslavement of women, which was fortunate for the Japanese government

---

[184] "Comfort Women." Wikipedia, Wikimedia Foundation, 30 Nov. 2023, en.wikipedia.org/wiki/Comfort_women.

given that an estimated ninety percent of the so-called comfort women perished and few women survived the conflict.[185]

Initially, the brothels were formed with the purpose of offering soldiers a means to satisfy their sexual desires, hence mitigating the occurrence of wartime sexual assault and the spread of sexually transmitted diseases. Paradoxically, the comfort stations had the opposite outcome, as they led to a rise in both sexual assaults and the transmission of sexually transmitted infections.

The initial victims were Japanese women, including both volunteers and those who were coerced or abducted through deceitful means. Later, due to a lack of Japanese volunteers and the need to protect Japan's reputation, the military turned to enlisting women from Japan's colonies. Women were often enticed by deceptive job ads for positions as nurses and factory workers. Additionally, many females were lured by the commitments of financial support for pursuing higher education. A substantial number of comfort women were minors.

Given the extensive and organized nature of prostitution in Japan, it was logical to anticipate the presence of military prostitution inside the Japanese armed forces. Carmen Argibay, a former Argentine Supreme Court Justice, claims that the Japanese government aimed to curb acts of extreme violence, such as the Rape of Nanking, by confining cases of rape and sexual abuse to military-controlled facilities. This strategy also aimed to prevent any such incidents from being reported to the international media. In addition, she maintains that the government aimed to reduce

---

[185] Blakemore, Erin. "The Brutal History of Japan's 'Comfort Women.'" History.Com, A&E Television Networks, 31 May 2023, www.history.com/news/comfort-women-japan-military-brothels-korea.

medical costs associated with treating venereal diseases contracted by soldiers through frequent and extensive instances of rape, hence impeding Japan's military capabilities. [186]

Military brothels, which had been present within the Japanese military since 1932, experienced significant growth after a notorious incident during imperial Japan's endeavor to conquer the Republic of China. Japanese forces initiated a six-week-long massacre on December 13, 1937, which essentially devastated the Chinese city of Nanking. Japanese forces sexually assaulted a staggering 20,000 to 80,000 Chinese women en route. The global community was appalled by the mass rapes, and Emperor Hirohito was apprehensive about how it would affect Japan's reputation.[187]

Comfort women had deplorable living conditions and were derogatorily referred to as "public toilets" by the Japanese. According to Yuki Tanaka, author of *Japan's Comfort Women* (2001), brothels located beyond the military's jurisdiction faced security concerns due to the potential presence of spies masquerading as prostitutes in these private establishments. Japanese historian, Yoshiaki Yoshimi, stated that the Japanese military employed comfort women as a means to appease dissatisfied soldiers during World War II and suppress any potential rebellion within the military.

During the initial phase of World War II, Japanese authorities employed traditional methods to enlist prostitutes. In urban areas, conventional advertising techniques that involved intermediaries were used alongside

---

[186] "Comfort Women." Wikipedia.
[187] Blakemore, Erin. "The Brutal History of Japan's 'Comfort Women.'"

abductions. The Ministry of Foreign Affairs eventually opposed granting additional travel visas to Japanese prostitutes, since they believed it would damage the reputation of the Japanese Empire. The military then resorted to procuring comfort women from regions outside mainland Japan, primarily from Korea and occupied China. Japan was able to easily recruit a significant number of women in Korea due to the presence of an established system of licensed prostitution.

A significant number of women were tricked or defrauded into working in the military brothels. Many Korean girls volunteered for the work, enticed by the prospect of receiving cash that may be utilized to reduce their family's financial obligations. Occasionally, brothel managers purchased Korean women for prices ranging from 300 to 1,000 yen, based on their physical attributes. These women would then become the manager's possessions and were not set free even after fulfilling the agreed-upon terms of servitude stated in the contract.

Due to the immense pressures of the war, the Japanese military reached a point where it was no longer capable of adequately supplying its divisions. Consequently, the units resorted to acquiring more supplies by either demanding them from or plundering them from the local population. Frequently, the military explicitly requested that local leaders acquire women for the brothels located near the battlefront, particularly in rural areas where intermediaries were scarce.

In his 1997 book "Korea's Place in the Sun: A Modern History," Bruce Cumings, an American historian specializing in East Asia, explicitly states that Japan implemented quotas to provide for the comfort women program, and that Korean men actively participated in the recruitment of victims. Cumings reports that an estimated 100,000 to 200,000 Korean girls and women were recruited. Daughters belonging to the upper class and government officials were exempted from being recruited in the "comfort women corps" unless they or their families demonstrated indications of supporting independence. The vast majority of Korean girls recruited into the comfort women corps were from impoverished backgrounds. The army and navy frequently delegated the task of recruiting females for the comfort women corps in Korea to subcontractors, typically affiliated with criminal syndicates, who received compensation for providing women. While a significant number of the contractors in Korea were of Japanese origin, the bulk were of Korean origin.

During the initial invasion of the Dutch East Indies, Japanese troops perpetrated several instances of sexual assault against Indonesian and European women and girls. The *Kenpeitai* (the military police of the Imperial Japanese Army) implemented the comfort women program as a means of managing the problem. The Kenpeitai coerced and deceived incarcerated women, including several hundred European women, into engaging in prostitution. Some women chose to live in the homes of Japanese commanders, assuming the role of a sexual slave to a single man, rather than catering to several men in a brothel.

According to J.F. van Wagtendonk and the Dutch Broadcast Foundation, approximately 400 Dutch girls were forcibly abducted from the refugee or prisoner of war camps in the Dutch East Indies to serve as comfort women. A comprehensive investigation done by the Dutch government provided a detailed account of the manipulative strategies utilized by the

Japanese military to forcefully subject women to sexual slavery.[188] Some individuals, confronted with extreme hunger in the camps, consented to receive food and compensation in exchange for work, the specifics of which were not fully disclosed to them. Several women also volunteered with the intention of safeguarding the younger women.

In addition to enduring daily and nightly acts of rape, the Dutch girls lived in a state of perpetual fear, dreading beatings and other forms of physical punishment. The women were forced into engaging in sexual acts with 10 soldiers on regular days and up to 40 soldiers on days after battles. To facilitate medical care for wounded Japanese soldiers, some of them were forced to contribute their blood. The women were not adequately provided with food, water, suitable lodging, toilets, and washing facilities. Furthermore, the medical care they received was restricted to addressing sexually transmitted illnesses, sterilization, and abortions. Women who tried to escape or resisted the troops' demands were subjected to torture. Moreover, there were occasions when the families of women who made suicide attempts were subjected to threats.

Since comfort women were forced to travel to the battlefields with the Japanese Imperial Army, many perished as Allied forces overwhelmed Japan's Pacific defenses and annihilated Japanese encampments. In certain instances, the Japanese military executed comfort women when they fled from losing battles with the Allied forces.[189]

---

[188] Ministerie van Buitenlandse zaken (January 24, 1994). "Gedwongen prostitutie van Nederlandse vrouwen in voormalig Nederlands-Indië [Enforced prostitution of Dutch women in the former Dutch East Indies]". Handelingen Tweede Kamer der Staten-Generaal [Hansard Dutch Lower House] (in Dutch). 23607 (1). ISSN 0921-7371. Archived from the original on September 27, 2007.
[189] "Comfort Women." Wikipedia, Wikimedia Foundation, 30 Nov. 2023, en.wikipedia.org/wiki/Comfort_women.

Jeanne Alida Ruff-O'Herne

Jeanne Alida "Jan" Ruff-O'Herne (1923–2019) was a Dutch Australian of Irish ancestry and a prominent advocate for human rights. She gained recognition for her global efforts in combatting the issue of wartime sexual violence.

Ruff-O'Herne was pressed into sexual servitude by the Imperial Japanese Army during World War II. She broke her silence after a period of fifty years and began actively advocating from the 1990s until her death. Her objectives were to demand an official apology from the Japanese government and to draw attention to the difficult circumstances faced by other comfort women.

Ruff-O'Herne was born in 1923 in Bandung in the Dutch East Indies, then a colony of the Dutch Empire. During the Japanese occupation of the Dutch East Indies, Ruff-O'Herne and thousands of Dutch women were forced to engage in arduous manual labor within a prisoner-of-war camp situated in an abandoned military facility at Ambarawa, Indonesia.

In February 1944, senior Japanese authorities visited the camp and instructed all unmarried girls aged seventeen and above to form a queue. Ten young women were selected, including twenty-one-year-old Ruff-O'Herne. Ruff-O'Herne and six other young women were taken by Japanese officers to an old Dutch colonial house at Semarang. The girls anticipated being coerced to engage in factory labor or exploited for propaganda purposes. They soon discovered that the colonial mansion was going to be transformed into a military brothel.

Photographs of the women were taken and exhibited at the reception area on the first day. The soldiers selected the girls they desired from the images. All the girls were assigned Japanese names, specifically names of flowers. During the course of three months, the women were repeatedly raped and beaten.

Ruff-O'Herne actively resisted the soldiers on a nightly basis and went as far as altering her appearance by cutting her hair to appear unattractive to the Japanese soldiers. Contrary to her expectation, her shorter hair length made her an object of interest.

Prior to the conclusion of World War II, the women were relocated to a camp situated in Bogor, West Java, where they were subsequently reunited with their families. The Japanese issued a warning, stating that revealing the details of their experiences would result in the execution of both the individuals involved and their immediate relatives. While some of the girls' parents made assumptions about what had happened, most opted to remain silent.

After the war ended, Ruff-O'Herne met Tom Ruff, a member of the British military. The couple married in 1946. In 1960, the couple left Britain for Australia, where they raised their two daughters.

Ruff-O'Herne had hinted at the wartime experiences she had endured and requested Tom's understanding and patience in their upcoming marriage in the letters she had sent to him. Following the war, Ruff-O'Herne experienced persistent nightmares and anxiety, particularly during intimate encounters with her husband. Despite having a strong marital bond, Ruff-O'Herne's life was persistently impacted by her traumatic experience as a comfort woman.

On February 15, 2007, Ruff-O'Herne spoke before the United States House of Representatives during a congressional hearing focused on "Protecting the Human Rights of Comfort Women." In her testimony, she stated:

> Many stories have been told about the horrors, brutalities, suffering and starvation of Dutch women in Japanese prison camps. But one story was never told, the most shameful story of the worst human rights abuse committed by the Japanese during World War II: The story of the comfort women, the *jugun ianfu*, and how these women were forcibly seized against their will to provide sexual services for the Japanese Imperial Army... I have forgiven the Japanese for what they did to me, but I can never forget. For fifty years, the comfort women maintained silence; they lived with a terrible shame, of feeling soiled and dirty. It has taken fifty years for these women's ruined lives to become a human rights issue. I hope that by speaking out, I have been able to make a contribution to world peace and reconciliation, and that human rights violations against women will never happen again. [190]

Ruff-O'Herne passed away in Adelaide on August 20, 2019, at the age of 96. The character Ellen Jansen in *Comfort Women: A New Musical* is based on Ruff-O'Herne.[191]

---

[190] "Jan Ruff O'Herne." Wikipedia, Wikimedia Foundation, 14 Oct. 2023, en.wikipedia.org/wiki/Jan_Ruff_O%27Herne.
[191] "Jan Ruff O'Herne." Wikipedia.

Prostitution Prevention Law

The *Prostitution Prevention Law*, also known as *Law No. 118* or the *Baishun boshi ho*, was passed on May 24, 1956. The legislation was enacted on April 1, 1957, and its aspects were fully in force on April 1 of the following year. The main objective of the law was to deter prostitution, penalize third-party individuals who participated in the business, and safeguard and rehabilitate women engaged in prostitution. However, since the law does not explicitly penalize the client and the prostitute, it is considered a preventive measure rather than a prohibitive law.

Starting in the late 1880s, some organizations, such as the international Woman's Christian Temperance Union and Purity Society, advocated for the abolition of legalized prostitution. The Japanese government opposed these proposals, arguing that legalized prostitution offered effective regulation of sexually transmitted infections and that without it, men's sexual urges would result in a rise in incidents of rape and sexual offenses. In response to the pressure exerted by the abolitionists, the Home Ministry said in May 1934 that licensed prostitution would be eliminated in the foreseeable future, however no concrete measures were implemented.

Prostitution continued to flourish during the period of American occupation in Japan after World War II. In January 1946, the General Headquarters of the Supreme Commander for the Allied Powers issued a directive to eliminate regulated prostitution. Consequently, the

Businesses Affecting Public Morals Regulation Act was enacted in 1948. A year earlier, a bill that aimed to abolish prostitution was introduced to Japan's *Diet* (parliament), but it was ultimately rejected.

However, female members of the Diet made multiple attempts to introduce different restrictions against prostitution until they finally achieved success with the enactment of the *Prostitution Prevention Law* in May 1956. Prime Minister Ichiro Hatoyama formed a *Council on Prostitution Policy*, led by Tsusai Sugawara, a prominent opponent of prostitution. The council drafted a law that made solicitation, procurement, and contracts for prostitution illegal, while the act of prostitution itself remained legal. Sugawara acknowledged that the compromise legislation had flaws, but it effectively prohibited the sale of daughters into prostitution.[192]

Typically, women view the passing of this law as a triumph in the journey towards women's freedom. It was achieved via the collaboration of women's organizations that joined forces to eliminate prostitution and the licensing system that supported it. Nevertheless, while the policy was being implemented, the sex workers in the red-light districts established a labor union and systematically protested against it until it was fully enforced in 1958. Advocates of the measure saw the acts of the prostitutes' unions as akin to extortion and bribes, considering them strategic tactics employed by individuals in the prostitution sector to guarantee its continuation. The prostitutes themselves were perceived as mere pawns, being used by their bosses without question. In the sixty plus years since the institution of the law, a huge adult entertainment industry has

---

[192] "Prostitution Prevention Law." Wikipedia, Wikimedia Foundation, 19 Mar. 2023, en.wikipedia.org/wiki/Prostitution_Prevention_Law.

continued to absorb destitute women and force them into prostitution much as before.[193]

The *Prostitution Prevention Law* explicitly prohibits only the exchange of money for vaginal intercourse, allowing for the permissibility of other sexual acts. Two prevalent contemporary iterations of Japan's brothels include *fasshonherusu* (fashion health) establishments and *sopurando* (soap lands). Fashion health centers are commonly promoted as massage parlors; however, they provide a wide range of services beyond mere massages. Indeed, the only aspect they are unable to provide is vaginal sexual intercourse. In this instance, strict adherence to the legal provisions is maintained.

Soap lands are facilities that offer the service of allowing customers to be bathed by partners of their choice. However, they offer a substantial proportion of the same services as brothels. They often exceed legal limits and devise methods to circumvent restrictions around prostitution on behalf of their clients. This is the prime example of the most intricate manipulation of a legal loophole. The law explicitly prohibits engaging in sexual activity with an unidentified individual in return for compensation. The crucial term in this context is "unidentified." Several soap lands, along with a few other sexual establishments, have managed to operate within the bounds of Japanese law by asserting that the sexual activity takes place between individuals who have established a personal connection and are no longer considered "unidentified."

---

[193] Yuki, Shiga-Fujime, and Beverly L. Findlay-Kaneko. "The Prostitutes' Union and the Impact of the 1956 Anti-Prostitution Law in Japan." U.S.-Japan Women's Journal. English Supplement, no. 5, 1993, pp. 3–27. JSTOR, http://www.jstor.org/stable/42772058. Accessed 16 Dec. 2023.

However, these adult industries are still subject to strict regulations. They are required to report to the police in order to register under specific designations, such as soap lands, fashion health massage parlors, call-girl businesses, strip clubs, love hotels, and adult shops. They are also legally obligated to operate exclusively within the chosen category. Nevertheless, numerous enterprises continue to exploit the language of the statute, rendering it impracticable to prosecute various types of prostitution. Prostitution may be regarded as *de facto legal* in many cases due to the pervasiveness of the semantic arguments around it.[194]

---

[194] Barrett, Rudy. "Japanese Legal Loopholes." Tofugu, Tofugu, 16 Oct. 2014, www.tofugu.com/japan/japanese-legal-loopholes/.

Glossary

Agedai Fee for engaging a prostitute.

Ageya Prior to the establishment of teahouses in the geisha districts, it served as an assignment house where men met with the high-ranking courtesans.

Akasen The Japanese slang phrase refers to districts that were historically involved in the sex work business in Japan, notably during the period from January 1946 to March 1958.

Aruki miko Literally "walking shrine maiden." Some of these women, compelled to endure destitution, resorted to prostitution as a viable option to survive.

Asobi The phrase "to play" is used to mean "to have a good time." The term used to refer to a group of Shinto priestesses who were involved in the practice of prostitution.

Baishun The term "selling youth" refers to the act of commodifying and profiting off the concept of youthfulness; it is a term used for prostitution.

Chigo	The acolytes, or monk apprentices, who also partook in same-sex relationships with elder monks.
Choya	Also known as "mune." The individual in charge of an asobi group who administered the group's organizational structure, safeguarded its members against unscrupulous clients, ensured group unity, and distributed the group's resources.
Haikai	A prevalent form of Japanese linked verse that originated in the sixteenth century from the antecedent aristocratic *renga*. Its meaning was "earthy" or "vulgar" and its effect was frequently achieved through satire and puns.
Imayo	The contemporary popular songs during the Heian period.
Kaishun	Engaging in the transactional exchange of sexual services.
Kamuro	The child attendants of the highest ranked courtesan.
Karayuki	The term "Miss Gone to China" refers to Japanese women who voluntarily, or involuntarily, migrated to different regions of the

	Asia-Pacific region to engage in occupations such as prostitution, being a courtesan, and geisha work.
Kashizashiki gyo	The term "room rental establishment" was used to refer to brothels after the implementation of the Prostitute Emancipation Act in 1872.
Kokyu	It is the only string instrument in traditional Japanese music that is played using a bow.
Koto	A Japanese plucked half-tube zither instrument, which is also the national instrument of Japan.
Kouta	Edo period traditional Japanese music that developed in red-light districts.
Kugutsu	Frequently misidentified as asobi, these women belonged to a nomadic society that included both male and female members. While both males and females engaged in puppetry, the females also participated in prostitution and sang imayo melodies.
Mawashibeya	Designated spaces within a shared large quarter where courtesans entertained their own clients.

Miko	A shrine maiden, or simply a young priestess, is an employee of a Shinto shrine. Originally considered to be shamans, these individuals now serve an institutionalized role in everyday Japanese society. They are trained to perform a variety of duties, including sacred purification and the sacred Kagura dance.
Myoseki	Generational names bestowed upon esteemed courtesans of great rank, such as oiran or tayu.
Najimi	The familiar or regular client of a courtesan.
Nanshoku	The Japanese phrase, alternatively pronounced as *danshaku*, is the Japanese rendition of the identical characters in Chinese, which directly translate to "male colors." The letter 色, which literally means "color," also has the connotation of "lust" in both China and Japan. This term was commonly employed to denote homoerotic activity between males throughout the pre-modern era of Japan.
Ochaya	In essence, a teahouse. An obsolete expression that originated during the Edo period, it denotes an establishment where customers are entertained by geisha.

Oiran	The word refers to the highest-ranking courtesans in Japanese history.
Okabasho	The term used to refer to the unauthorized red-light districts in Japan.
Okiya	The lodging house to which a maiko or geisha is affiliated with during her career.
Orandayuki	The term used to refer to the prostitutes who provided services to the Dutch in Nagasaki.
Renga	Japanese collaborative poetry in which numerous poets link alternating stanzas in succession.
Sado	Japanese tea ceremony.
Shakuhachi	A Japanese bamboo flute that is played by blowing into one end.
Shamisen	A three-stringed traditional Japanese musical instrument originating from the Chinese sanxian instrument.
Shinzo	The apprentice courtesans.

Showake	The appropriate conduct and protocols that a consumer should adhere to when engaging with sex workers.
Shuudo	Literally means "way of youth" and has been employed to encompass several aspects of same-sex relationships in Japan, including priest-acolyte connections, male prostitution, as well as artistic and literary works that explore the unique affinity between adult males and youths.
Suri-ashi	The distinctive sliding, figure eight step the oiran executed with her high koma geta during the oiran parade.
Ukiyo	The concept of the "floating world" refers to the hedonistic qualities of Japan during the Edo period.
Wakaimono	The manservants who assisted in maintaining the oiran's balance as she performed the oiran dochu.
Yujo	Prostitutes, commonly referred to as "women of pleasure."
Yukaku	The phrase "play house" refers to the authorized areas for prostitution in Japan.

Zegen   An individual who earns their livelihood by engaging in the commercial activity of trafficking women into the sex trade.

List of Illustrations

i. A kamuro having makeup applied, photo by Yoshiro Miyazaki, public domain 8

ii. Abe Sada circa 1947, public domain 2

iii. Illustration from "Complete Set of Fifty-four Chapters of the Tale of Genji" by Ogata Gekkō, 1893, public domain 10

iv. Aruki miko depicted on a six-panel folding screen from "Views in and around Kyoto" ("Rakuchu-Rakugai zu"), circa 1660, artist unknown, public domain 12

v. Izumo no Okuni, by an anonymous artist from the school of Matabei Kan'ei Era (1624-1644), part of a six-panel screen, public domain 16

vi. Izumo no Okuni on stage as depicted in the illustrated manuscript KUNIJO KABUKI EKOTOBA (Kuni's Kabuki), public domain 20

vii. Fragment of the "Illustrated Life of Priest Honen," 13th to early 14th century, depicts an asobi trio in their boat approaching the priest sent to exile in Tosa, public domain 22

viii. Shizuka Gozen by Katsushika Hokusai, circa 1825, public domain 30

ix. Second-Floor Parlor in New Yoshiwara by Okumura Masanobu, circa 1745, public domain 36

x. Ground-plan of the Dutch trade-post on the island Dejima at Nagasaki by Isaac Titsingh circa 1824-1825, public domain 42

xi. Map of Yoshiwara 1846, public domain 44

xii. Mikaeri Yanagi by Utagawa Hiroshige, circa 1853, public domain 45

xiii. New Year's Day at the Ōgiya Brothel, Yoshiwara by Katsushika Hokusai circa 1804, panel 1, public domain 49

xiv. New Year's Day at the Ōgiya Brothel, Yoshiwara by Katsushika Hokusai circa 1804, panel 2, public domain 50

xv. New Year's Day at the Ōgiya Brothel, Yoshiwara by Katsushika Hokusai, circa 1804, panel 3, public domain 51

xvi. New Year's Day at the Ōgiya Brothel, Yoshiwara by Katsushika Hokusai, circa 1804, panel 4, public domain 52

xvii. New Year's Day at the Ōgiya Brothel, Yoshiwara by Katsushika Hokusai, circa 1804, panel 5, public domain 53

xviii. No. 9 Nectarine Brothel, Yoshiwara, circa 1910, public domain 57
xix. Sano Jirozaemon Murdering a Courtesan (1886), by Tsukioka Yoshitoshi, left panel, public domain.. 58
xx. The main gate of Jokan-ji... 62
xxi. Crypt honoring the twenty-five thousand prostitutes, Jokan-ji................. 65
xxii. Willow Tree at the Gate of the Shimabara Pleasure Quarter from the series "Famous Places in Kyoto"by Utagawa Hiroshige, circa 1834, public domain 66
xxiii. Nakanoshima in Osaka. Creative Commons Attribution-Share Alike 4.0 International license... 70
xxiv. The Bizen-ya teahouse in Furuichi, Ise, circa 1890s, photographer unknown, public domain.. 73
xxv. The actors Fujikawa Tomokichi II and Onoe Matsusuke II playing the roles of the courtesan Okon and Fukuoka Mitsugi by Utagawa Kunisada I, panel 1, public domain.. 76
xxvi. The actors Fujikawa Tomokichi II and Onoe Matsusuke II playing the roles of the courtesan Okon and Fukuoka Mitsugi by Utagawa Kunisada I, panel 2, public domain.. 77
xxvii. The lover's grave at Dairin-ji Temple, Furuichi............................... 81
xxviii. Maruyama brothel, circa 1890s, public domain.................................. 84
xxix. Lower-level prostitutes displayed in wooden latticed cages known as harimise in Yoshiwara, circa 1889, photographer unknown, public domain . 104
xxx. Men entering the Nectarine No. 9 brothel in Yoshiwara with prostitutes standing on the balconies, circa 1889, photographer unknown, public domain
.... 104
xxxi. Satogiku Dayu with kamuro, circa 1910, public domain 105
xxxii. Oiran dochu, Yoshiwara, circa 1920, public domain......................... 111
xxxiii. Takao Dayu II by Utagawa Hiroshige, (1797-1858), public domain .. 119
xxxiv. Ukiyo-e print depicting Date Tsunamune slaying Takao Dayu, artist unknown, public domain... 122
xxxv. Portrait of Date Tsunamune, artist unknown, public domain............... 123
xxxvi. The Courtesan Usugumo Holding a Cat by Tsukioka Yoshitoshi, circa 1876, public domain 124
xxxvii. Yoshino Tayu (2nd generation), Joshoji Temple collection, public domain 127
xxxviii. Komurasaki Dayu by Hosoda Eishi, circa 1794, public domain....... 131

xxxix. Ito Hirobumi as prime minister, circa 1880s, public domain 135
xl. Karayuki-san in Saigon, circa 1910, public domain 140
xli. Yamada Waka and her husband, Kakichi, public domain 146
xlii. Portrait of Ine's mother Kusumoto Taki, circa the 1830s, public domain 152
xliii. Philipp Franz Balthasar von Siebold, public domain 153
xliv. Photo of Kusumoto Ine, public domain 156
xlv. Hell Courtesan (Jigoku dayû) by Kawanabe Kyōsai circa the 1870s-1880s, public domain 160
xlvi. Samurai and Male Youth by Miyagawa Issho, early 18th century, public domain 162
xlvii. Yasuura House (Recreation and Amusement Association) brothel in Yokosuka City, circa 1945-46, public domain 172
xlviii. Jan Ruff O'Herne (Bandoengan, Java, 1942), public domain 179

Works Cited

Works in English:

"1855 Edo Earthquake." Wikipedia, 14 May 2023, en.wikipedia.org/wiki/1855_Edo_earthquake#:~:text=The%201855%20Edo%20earthquake%20(%E5%AE%89%E6%94%BF, local%20time%20on%2011%20November.

Aarsman, Mieke. "Omiai: Love and Sex in Ancient Japan." Tokiotours: Your Personal Tour Guide in Tokyo, 14 July 2013, tokiotours.wordpress.com/2013/07/14/omiai-love-and-sex-in-ancient-japan/.

"Akasen." Wikipedia, Wikimedia Foundation, 12 June 2022, en.wikipedia.org/wiki/Akasen.

"Asobi (Ancient Japan)." Wikipedia, 4 June 2023, en.wikipedia.org/wiki/Asobi_(ancient_Japan).

Barrett, Rudy. "Japanese Legal Loopholes." Tofugu, Tofugu, 16 Oct. 2014, www.tofugu.com/japan/japanese-legal-loopholes/.

Blakemore, Erin. "The Brutal History of Japan's 'Comfort Women.'" History.Com, A&E Television Networks, 31 May 2023, www.history.com/news/comfort-women-japan-military-brothels-korea.

Cartwright, Mark. "Ise Grand Shrine." World History Encyclopedia, https://www.worldhistory.org#organization, 15 Sept. 2023, www.worldhistory.org/Ise_Grand_Shrine/.

Choi, Eunice. "Kyoto: Pleasure Quarters." Kyoto: Architecture 1562-1657, www.columbia.edu/itc/ealac/V3613/kyoto/recreational/pleasure.html. Accessed 25 Sept. 2023.

Clark, Austin. "Concubinage in Asia." Women's History Resource Site, 18 Dec. 2001, departments.kings.edu/womens_history/concubin.html#:~:text=The%20rich%20and%20the%20ruling,emotional%20fulfillment%2C%20and%20sexual%20pleasure.

"Comfort Women." Wikipedia, Wikimedia Foundation, 30 Nov. 2023, en.wikipedia.org/wiki/Comfort_women.

"Complete Guide: Jokanji Temple (Arakawa, Tokyo)." *The Tokyo Shitamachi Guide*, 15 May 2023, everywhere.tokyo/en/jokanji-temple/.

"Courtesans." Courtesans - SamuraiWiki, samurai-archives.com/w/index.php?title=Courtesans&mobileaction=toggle_view_desktop. Accessed 2 Feb. 2024.

"Dairinji." Dairinji - SamuraiWiki, 2010, samurai-archives.com/wiki/Dairinji.

"Date Tsunamune." Wikipedia, 2 Feb. 2021, en.wikipedia.org/wiki/Date_Tsunamune.

"Dejima." Wikipedia, Wikimedia Foundation, 12 Nov. 2023, en.wikipedia.org/wiki/Dejima.

"Dejima: Nagasaki's 400-Year-Old Dutch Trading Post." Japanistry.Com, 13 Oct. 2021, www.japanistry.com/dejima/.

Downer, Lesley. "Women of the Pleasure Quarters-The Secret History of the Geisha." *The New York Times*, The New York Times, 2001, archive.nytimes.com/www.nytimes.com/books/first/d/downer-01pleasure.html.

"Edo Period." Wikipedia, Wikimedia Foundation, 21 Sept. 2023, en.wikipedia.org/wiki/Edo_period.

Edwards, Meradeth Lin. *Professional Heartbreakers: Male Entertainers and the Divide Between Popular Culture and History in Japan.* University of San Diego - Digital USD, 2018, digital.sandiego.edu/cgi/viewcontent.cgi?article=1030&context=theses.

"The Fifty-Three Stations of the Tōkaidō." Wikipedia, Wikimedia Foundation, 27 Aug. 2023, en.wikipedia.org/wiki/The_Fifty-three_Stations_of_the_T%C5%8Dkaid%C5%8D.

"Forgotten Foibles: Love and the Dutch at Dejima (1641–1854)." Forgotten Foibles: Love and the Dutch at Dejima (1641–1854) | East Asian History, 2021, www.eastasianhistory.org/39/vos-foibles/index.html.

"Furuichi." Furuichi - SamuraiWiki, 2010, samurai-archives.com/wiki/Furuichi.

Geimaiko. "The Figure Eight Walk." GeiMaiko, 19 July 2020, geimaiko.tumblr.com/post/624055474380210176/the-figure-eight-walk#:~:text=Oiran%20%2D%20Soto%20Hachi%20Monji&text=The%20Oiran's%20walking%20style%20is,damage%20to%20her%20expensive%20footwear.

"History of Prostitution." Wikipedia, Wikimedia Foundation, 15 Mar. 2023, https://en.wikipedia.org/wiki/History_of_prostitution#:~:text=Ancient%20Near%20East,-See%20also%3A%20Sacred&text=2400%20BCE%20are%20the%20earliest,in%20the%20city%20of%20Uruk.

Hix, Lisa. "Sex and Suffering: The Tragic Life of the Japanese Courtesan." Ms. Magazine, 19 July 2018, msmagazine.com/2015/03/27/sex-and-suffering-the-tragic-life-of-the-japanese-courtesan/.

Hyland, Meg. "Kokannon." Women of 1000 AD, 25 June 2020, womenof1000ad.weebly.com/kokannon.html.

"Ikkyū." Wikipedia, Wikimedia Foundation, 17 Dec. 2023, en.wikipedia.org/wiki/Ikky%C5%AB.

Iles, Stuart. "The Throw Away Temple – Dumping Ground of the Yoshiwara Prostitutes." Japanese History and Culture: Educational Studies of Japanese History, 5 Feb. 2015, rekishinihon.com/2015/02/06/the-throw-away-temple-dumping-ground-of-the-yoshiwara-prostitutes/.

"Ise, Mie." Wikipedia, Wikimedia Foundation, 23 June 2023, en.wikipedia.org/wiki/Ise,_Mie.

Issendai. "Kamuro." Kamuro | Japanese Courtesans | Issendai.Com, 2013, www.issendai.com/japanese-courtesans/kamuro.html.

"Izumo No Okuni." Wikipedia, Wikimedia Foundation, 30 Aug. 2023, en.wikipedia.org/wiki/Izumo_no_Okuni.

"Jan Ruff O'Herne." Wikipedia, Wikimedia Foundation, 14 Oct. 2023, en.wikipedia.org/wiki/Jan_Ruff_O%27Herne.

"Kabuki." Wikipedia, Wikimedia Foundation, 12 Nov. 2023, en.wikipedia.org/wiki/Kabuki.

"Kagema." Wikipedia, Wikimedia Foundation, 29 Apr. 2023, en.wikipedia.org/wiki/Kagema.

"Kamuro." Kamuro | Japanese Courtesans | Issendai.Com, 2013, www.issendai.com/japanese-courtesans/kamuro.html.

"Karayuki-San." Wikipedia, Wikimedia Foundation, 20 July 2023, en.wikipedia.org/wiki/Karayuki-san.

Keohan, Matt. "These Are the Top 10 Countries That Spend the Most on Prostitutes." BroBible, 13 Oct. 2022, brobible.com/life/article/top-10-countries-spend-most-prostitutes/.

Kim, Yung-Hee. "Songs to Make the Dust Dance: The Ryojin Hisho of Twelfth-Century Japan." Songs to Make the Dust Dance, 1994, publishing.cdlib.org/ucpressebooks/view?docId=ft2f59n7x0&chunk.id=d0e769&; toc.id=d0e769&; brand=ucpress.

Kirwan, Christy. "Women in the Heian Court: Wives, Concubines, and Lovers." Owlcation, 19 July 2022, owlcation.com/humanities/Women-in-the-Heian-Court.

Kobayashi, Akira. "The Courtesans of Yoshiwara." Nippon.Com, 20 Apr. 2022, www.nippon.com/en/japan-topics/g01083/.

Kuly, Lisa. "Locating Transcendence in Japanese Minzoku Geinô: Yamabushi and Miko Kagura – Ethnologies." Érudit, Association Canadienne d'Ethnologie et de Folklore, 20 Oct. 2003, www.erudit.org/en/journals/ethno/2003-v25-n1-ethno557/007130ar/.

"Kusumoto Ine." Wikipedia, 13 Sept. 2021, en.wikipedia.org/wiki/Kusumoto_Ine.

Lloyd, George. "What Became of Yoshiwara, Tokyo's Old Red-Light District?" Japan Today, 23 June 2020, japantoday.com/category/features/travel/what-became-of-yoshiwara-tokyo%E2%80%99s-old-red-light-district.

Lublin, Elizabeth D. "Sex Work During the Tokugawa Era." Oxford Research Encyclopedia of Asian History, 15 Sept. 2022, https://oxfordre.com/asianhistory/display/10.1093/acrefore/9780190277727.001.0001/acrefore-9780190277727-e-71;jsessionid=B0531C4D400EDF58D9F8BF7CC646B89C?rskey=oNrWlx&result=5.

"Marriage in Japan." Wikiwand, www.wikiwand.com/en/Marriage_in_Japan. Accessed 12 May 2023.

"Maruyama." Maruyama - SamuraiWiki, 2016, samurai-archives.com/wiki/Maruyama.

Matsuura, Thersa. "Jigoku Tayuu: The Mysterious Hell Courtesan (Ep. 74)." Uncanny Japan Podcast, 15 Apr. 2021, uncannyjapan.com/podcast/jigoku-tayuu/.

Matsuura, Thersa. "Oiran: The Glamorous and Wretched Life of a High Courtesan (Ep. 61)." Uncanny Japan Podcast, 1 Oct. 2020, uncannyjapan.com/podcast/oiran-high-courtesan/.

McNeill, Maggie. "Takao." The Honest Courtesan, 24 Mar. 2015, maggiemcneill.com/2015/03/24/takao/.

"Miko." Wikipedia, Wikimedia Foundation, 24 Oct. 2023, en.wikipedia.org/wiki/Miko.

Ministerie van Buitenlandse zaken (January 24, 1994). "Gedwongen prostitutie van Nederlandse vrouwen in voormalig Nederlands-Indië [Enforced prostitution of Dutch women in the former Dutch East Indies]". Handelingen Tweede Kamer der Staten-Generaal [Hansard Dutch Lower House].

Nyugen. "Usugumo Tayu: Tama, The Calico Cat from Which the Maneki Neko Is Derived." RSS, 24 Apr. 2019, monspedia.com/usugumo/.

Ohkubo, Kristine. *Nickname Flower of Evil* (呼び名は悪の花): *The Abe Sada Story*. 2019.

Ohkubo, Kristine. "The Substitute Dog (Okage-Inu) - Japanup! Magazine." JapanUp! Magazine - Informational Site for Japan Fans, 28 Sept. 2022, japanupmagazine.com/archives/6989?fbclid=IwAR0hN6J0IudXCtNHRyipus_mFIhTco gj3WR9Tbg_80igy8IRH8Xve3_V5Sc.

"Oiran." Wikipedia, 22 Apr. 2023, en.wikipedia.org/wiki/Oiran.

"Prostitution in Japan." Wikipedia, Wikimedia Foundation, 28 Dec. 2022, https://en.wikipedia.org/wiki/Prostitution_in_Japan.

"Prostitution Prevention Law." Wikipedia, Wikimedia Foundation, 19 Mar. 2023, en.wikipedia.org/wiki/Prostitution_Prevention_Law.

"Recreation and Amusement Association." Wikipedia, 22 Mar. 2023, en.wikipedia.org/wiki/Recreation_and_Amusement_Association.

Richie, Donald. "KAGOTSURUBE." Kabuki21, www.kabuki21.com/kagotsurube.php. Accessed 16 Sept. 2023.

"Sacred Prostitution." Wikipedia, Wikimedia Foundation, 15 Feb. 2023, https://en.wikipedia.org/wiki/Sacred_prostitution.

Sakowako, Y. "20 Facts You Did Not Know about Oiran." Tsunagu Japan, 2015, www.tsunagujapan.com/20-facts-you-did-not-know-about-oiran/.

Seigle, Cecilia Segawa. "Corporal Punishment and Other Abuses." *Yoshiwara: The Glittering World of the Japanese Courtesan*, University of Hawaii, Honolulu, HI, 1993.

"Sharebon." Wikipedia, 4 Mar. 2023, en.wikipedia.org/wiki/Sharebon.

"Shimabara, Kyoto." Wikipedia, Wikimedia Foundation, 26 Sept. 2023, en.wikipedia.org/wiki/Shimabara,_Kyoto.

"Shinmachi." Wikipedia, 12 Oct. 2022, en.wikipedia.org/wiki/Shinmachi.

"Shirabyōshi." Wikipedia, Wikimedia Foundation, 11 Jan. 2024, en.wikipedia.org/wiki/Shiraby%C5%8Dshi.

"Shizuka Gozen." Wikipedia, Wikimedia Foundation, 12 Jan. 2023, en.wikipedia.org/wiki/Shizuka_Gozen.

Squires, Graham. "Edo Period." World History Encyclopedia, 11 Oct. 2022, www.worldhistory.org/Edo_Period/.

Stanley, Amy. "Regulation and the Logic of the Household." Selling Women: Prostitution, Markets, and the Household in Early Modern Japan, University of California Press, Berkeley, 2012, p. 80.

Sugoii Japan. "Yoshiwara - Discover the Old Tokyo Red Light District of Edo Period." Sugoii Japan, 20 Apr. 2022, sugoii-japan.com/yoshiwara-tokyo-old-red-light-district.

"Takao II." Wikipedia, 12 Mar. 2023, en.wikipedia.org/wiki/Takao_II.

"The Tragic Lives of the 5 Most Famous Oiran - Can You Imagine the Cruel Truth? - With En Subtitles." YouTube, 27 Aug. 2022, www.youtube.com/watch?v=_Y5vc8MmgNE.

"Tsujigiri." Wikipedia, Wikimedia Foundation, 19 June 2023, en.wikipedia.org/wiki/Tsujigiri.

Weber, Zoe. "From Courtesan to Geisha by Zoe Weber." ON EAST, 2014, https://oneast.sa.utoronto.ca/publication/2013-14/essays/from_courtesan_to_geisha/.

"Who Is Usugumo Dayu?" Shogakukan Encyclopedia of Japan (Nipponica), kotobank.jp/word/%E8%96%84%E9%9B%B2%E5%A4%AA%E5%A4%AB-1508015. Accessed 18 May 2023.

Writers, YABAI. "Miko: The Shrine Maidens of Japan." Yabai YABAI, 27 June 2017, http://yabai.com/p/2317.

"Yamada Waka." Wikipedia, 11 June 2023, en.wikipedia.org/wiki/Yamada_Waka.

"Yoshiwara." Wikipedia, 30 Apr. 2023, en.wikipedia.org/wiki/Yoshiwara.

Yu, A. C. "Imayo (A Popular Style of Japanese Songs in the Heian Period) - Japanese Wiki Corpus." Imayo (a Popular Style of Japanese Songs in the Heian Period) - Japanese Wiki Corpus, www.japanesewiki.com/culture/Imayo%20(a%20popular%20style%20of%20Japanese%20songs%20in%20the%20Heian%20period).html. Accessed 10 July 2023.

Yu, A. C. "Tekiya - Japanese Wiki Corpus." Tekiya - Japanese Wiki Corpus, www.japanesewiki.com/culture/Tekiya.html. Accessed 21 Feb. 2024.

Yu, A. C. "Wachigaiya (the Name of a Tea House) - Japanese Wiki Corpus." Wachigaiya (the Name of a Tea House) - Japanese Wiki Corpus, www.japanesewiki.com/building/Wachigaiya%20(the%20name%20of%20a%20tea%20house).html. Accessed 16 Dec. 2023.

Yu, A. C. "Yachiyo Tayu - Japanese Wiki Corpus." Yachiyo Tayu - Japanese Wiki Corpus, www.japanesewiki.com/person/Yachiyo%20tayu.html. Accessed 4 Jan. 2024.

Yu, A. C. "Yoshino Tayu (a Courtesan of the Highest Rank) - Japanese Wiki Corpus." Yoshino Tayu (a Courtesan of the Highest Rank) - Japanese Wiki Corpus, www.japanesewiki.com/literature/Yoshino%20Tayu%20(a%20courtesan%20of%20the%20highest%20rank).html. Accessed 18 May 2023.

Yuki, Shiga-Fujime, and Beverly L. Findlay-Kaneko. "The Prostitutes' Union and the Impact of the 1956 Anti-Prostitution Law in Japan." U.S.-Japan Women's Journal. English Supplement, no. 5, 1993, pp. 3–27. JSTOR, http://www.jstor.org/stable/42772058. Accessed 16 Dec. 2023.

Works in Japanese:

"油屋騒動 (Aburaya Riot)." Wikipedia, Wikimedia Foundation, 24 Apr. 2023, ja.wikipedia.org/wiki/%E6%B2%B9%E5%B1%8B%E9%A8%92%E5%8B%95.

"梅毒に感染も。江戸時代における遊女の一生が過酷すぎる【写真あり】| 江戸ガイド ("Also Infected with Syphilis. The Life of a Prostitute in the Edo Period Was Extremely Harsh [with Photos] | Edo Guide.") 江戸ガイド, 江戸ガイド, 9 Apr. 2022, edo-g.com/blog/2016/02/yujo.html.

Makino, Hiromi. "裁かれたのは誰なのか 吉原の遊女16人、集団放火その後/ Who Was Judged after the Mass Arson of 16 Yoshiwara Prostitutes?" 毎日新聞, 毎日新聞/ Mainichi Shimbun, 6 Oct. 2021, mainichi.jp/articles/20211005/k00/00m/040/161000c.

松島遊廓." (Matsushima red light district), Wikipedia, Wikimedia Foundation, 5 Sept. 2023, ja.wikipedia.org/wiki/%E6%9D%BE%E5%B3%B6%E9%81%8A%E5%BB%93.

"投げ込み寺 (Nagekomidera)." Wikipedia, 16 Aug. 2020, ja.wikipedia.org/wiki/%E6%8A%95%E3%81%92%E8%BE%BC%E3%81%BF%E5%AF%BA.

"佐野次郎左衛門 (Sano Jirozaemon)." Wikipedia, Wikimedia Foundation, 3 Sept. 2022, ja.wikipedia.org/wiki/%E4%BD%90%E9%87%8E%E6%AC%A1%E9%83%8E%E5%B7%A6%E8%A1%9B%E9%96%80.

"島原 (京都) (Shimabara (Kyoto))." Wikipedia, Wikimedia Foundation, 11 June 2023, ja.wikipedia.org/wiki/%E5%B3%B6%E5%8E%9F_(%E4%BA%AC%E9%83%BD).

"新町遊廓 (Shinmachi Red Light District)." Wikipedia, Wikimedia Foundation, 6 Sept. 2023, ja.wikipedia.org/wiki/%E6%96%B0%E7%94%BA%E9%81%8A%E5%BB%93.

"大橋太夫." (Tayu Ohashi). Wikipedia, Wikimedia Foundation, 15 June 2021, ja.wikipedia.org/wiki/%E5%A4%A7%E6%A9%8B%E5%A4%AA%E5%A4%AB.

"桜木太夫 (Tayu Sakuragi)." Wikipedia, Wikimedia Foundation, 6 Nov. 2022, ja.wikipedia.org/wiki/%E6%A1%9C%E6%9C%A8%E5%A4%AA%E5%A4%AB.

"吉原で最も有名な遊女「高尾太夫」と「16人の遊女たちの集団放火事件」/ Yoshiwara's Most Famous Prostitute, 'Tayu Takao' and the 'Mass Arson Incident of 16 Prostitutes.'" 草の実堂, 16 July 2022, kusanomido.com/study/history/japan/edo/59808/.

"夕霧太夫 (Yugiri Dayu I)." Wikipedia, Wikimedia Foundation, 11 July 2021, ja.wikipedia.org/wiki/%E5%A4%95%E9%9C%A7%E5%A4%AA%E5%A4%AB.

"遊女 (Yujo)." Wikipedia, Wikimedia Foundation, 15 Aug. 2023, ja.wikipedia.org/wiki/%E9%81%8A%E5%A5%B3.

About the Author

KRISTINE OHKUBO is a Los Angeles-based author whose work emphasizes topics related to Japan and Japanese culture. During her childhood in Chicago, she cultivated a deep reverence and affection for Japanese culture, people, and history. Through her many travels, she has gained unique insights into this fascinating country, which she shares in her books and various writings.

Published in 2016 (revised edition in 2022), her debut book was an anthology of numerous travel blog articles pertaining to Japan. In 2017, she released a historical examination of the Pacific War, focusing on the perspective of Japanese and Japanese American civilians living in Japan and the United States when the conflict began. Two years later, she supplemented her earlier works with the account of an infamous twentieth-century geisha who was both the aggressor and the victim, enduring a strict patriarchal culture and a rapidly changing social system. 2019 marked the publication of *Sakhalin*, a sequel to her 2017 book, *The Sun Will Rise Again*. With an emphasis on the tragic events that took place in August 1945, this book examines the far-reaching effects that the island's transfer of ownership had on its inhabitants and resources.

Kristine shifted her attention in 2020 to rakugo, the 400-year-old Japanese narrative art form. She released two books, *Talking About Rakugo 1: The Japanese Art of Storytelling* followed by *Talking About Rakugo 2: The Stories Behind the Storytellers*. By employing a combination of biographical information, anecdotes, interviews, and rakugo scripts, the author offers an exhaustive account of the enduring nature of this traditional art form. In 2022, Kristine contributed her editorial skills to an additional rakugo book authored by English rakugo storyteller Kanariya Eiraku and entitled *Eiraku's 100 English Rakugo Scripts (Volume 1)*. Following its publication in August, she undertook a reevaluation of a work that she had authored and published three years prior.

Asia's Masonic Reformation: Freemasonry's Impact on the Westernization and Subsequent Modernization of Asia, first published in January 2019, delves into the historical significance of Freemasons as catalysts of change in Asia and other regions. By presenting compelling historical evidence and specific examples, the revised second edition establishes that Freemasons had a significant impact on progress, enlightenment, and modernization. This is accomplished by conducting exhaustive research while ignoring the proliferation of false information and conspiracy theories that have developed over time.

Kristine, a dedicated rakugo devotee, realigned her focus towards the art form in 2023. She released a collection comprising her own unique English rakugo narratives and contributed to the editing and publication of *Eiraku's 100 English Rakugo Scripts (Volume 2)*.

As an author, Kristine believes that writing from other cultural perspectives encourages empathy and understanding, and at the same time it broadens our knowledge of the events that have unfolded over the years.

Nickname Flower of Evil (呼び名は悪の花): The Abe Sada Story

Paperback – September 17, 2019

Product details:

Language: English

Paperback: 162 pages

ISBN-10: 0578551470

ISBN-13: 978-0578551470

www.ingramcontent.com/pod-product-compliance
Lightning Source LLC
LaVergne TN
LVHW061035070526
838201LV00073B/5036